Restructuring Schools

Capturing and Assessing the Phenomena

JOSEPH MURPHY

TEACHERS
COLLEGE
PRESS

Teachers College, Columbia University
New York and London

Published by Teachers College Press, 1234 Amsterdam Avenue
New York, NY 10027

Support for this research was provided by the National Center for Educational Leadership (NCEL) under U.S. Department of Education Contract No. R 117C8005. The views in this report are those of the author
and do not necessarily represent those of the sponsoring institution nor
the Universities in the NCEL Consortium—The University of Chicago,
Harvard University, and Vanderbilt University.

Murphy, Joseph, 1949–
    Restructuring schools: capturing and assessing the phenomena /
Joseph Murphy.
    p. cm.
    Includes bibliographical references (p.) and index.
    ISBN 0-8077-3112-9. — ISBN 0-8077-3111-0 (pbk.)
    1. Educational change—United States.   2. School management and
organization—United States.   3. Schools—United States—
Decentralization.   I. Title.
LA217.2.M87   1991   91-4330
371.2'00973—dc20   CIP

Printed on acid-free paper

Manufactured in the United States of America

97   96   95   94   93   8   7   6   5   4   3   2

to
Linda C. Holste
my angel

Contents

Contents

Introduction

*President Bush and the nation's governors walked away
from last week's educational summit with an unprecedented agreement to establish national performance goals
and to engineer a radical restructuring of America's educational system. (Miller, 1989, October 4, p. 1)*

In the early 1980s, a concerted effort to reform American public
education began. The impetus for these attempts was primarily
economic. Analysts from all walks of society concluded that the
United States was on the verge of being displaced as a major
player in the world economy. The belief that we were falling behind other industrial powers in development, productivity, and
quality (Underwood, 1990) was a theme that laced the pages of
the various reform reports (see, for example, Carnegie Forum,
1986; Education Commission of the States, 1983; National Commission on Excellence in Education, 1983; National Governors' Association, 1986; National Science Board, 1983; for a review, see
Murphy, 1990a). It did not take reformers long to draw the connection between this economic impotence and the educational system. Nor was the potential for schooling to restore the economic
preeminence of the United States ignored:

> Sinking economic productivity, national debt, international com-
> mercial competition, trade deficits, and a declining dollar placed the
> nation in increasing economic jeopardy. Schooling was seen as part
> of the problem and part of the solution. (Guthrie & Kirst, 1988, p. 4;
> see also Association for Supervision and Curriculum Development,
> 1986; Kearnes, 1988a, 1988b)

Once the failure of schools to produce literate and numerate
graduates was documented (see Murphy, 1990a), and this short-
coming was inexorably linked to our declining economic position

in the world marketplace, investigators began dissecting the educational system in search of explanations. The fundamental conclusion of these analyses (see, for example, Boyer, 1983; Chubb, 1988; Goodlad, 1984; Powell, Farrar, & Cohen, 1985; Sedlak, Wheeler, Pullin, & Cusick, 1986; Sizer, 1984) was that schools were characterized by intellectual softness, a lack of expectations and standards, inadequate leadership, a dysfunctional organizational structure, conditions of employment inconsistent with professional work, and the absence of any meaningful accountability. When the system was laid open to review, the basic infrastructure was found to be in need of serious repair. The luster had worn off the educational enterprise.

The concern ensuing from these analyses, in conjunction with the original economic fears, launched the most widespread, intense, public, comprehensive, and sustained effort to improve education in our history (McCarthy, 1990; Murphy, 1990a; Odden & Marsh, 1988). Fueled by a plethora of commissioned national and state reform reports,[1] attempts to strengthen the quality of American public education began to unfold in states, districts, and schools throughout the nation. Initial, or wave 1 (1982–1986),[2] reform efforts focused on restoring quality by fixing the existing educational system (see Murphy, 1989a, 1990a for reviews). The philosophical infrastructure of early suggestions for repair was highly mechanistic, consisting mainly of centralized controls and standards (Boyd, 1987; Sedlak et al., 1986). The assumptions embedded in this approach suggest that the conditions of schooling contributing to poor student outcome measures are attributable to the poor quality of the workers and the inadequacy of their tools and that they are subject to revision through mandated, top-down initiatives—especially those from the state. Use of the bureaucratic model to institute improvement proposals led in turn to the emphasis in early reform efforts on policy mechanisms such as prescriptions, tightly specified resource allocations, and performance measurements that focused on repairing components of the system (e.g., writing better textbooks) and raising the quality of the workforce by telling employees how to work (e.g., specifying instructional models) (see Coombs, 1987; Hawley, 1988; Underwood, 1990). Reform initiatives in a dizzying array were discussed in reform reports and studies and subsequently passed into law by the various states (see Murphy, 1990b).

For a variety of reasons, which I treat in detail later, criticisms of these early efforts to reform schooling were quickly forthcoming (see, for example, Chubb, 1988; Cuban, 1984; Elmore, 1987; Purpel, 1989; Sedlak et al., 1986; Sizer, 1984). The consensus among critics of wave 1 reform measures was that they were taking educators down the wrong road, the road of the quick fix, and were using inappropriate policy tools to improve schooling, especially mandates from the top. These reformers argued that fundamental revisions were needed in the cultural institutions of the larger society, in the ways that educational systems were organized and governed, in the roles adults played in schools, and in the processes used to educate America's youth. The belief that the current system was beyond repair began to take root. Analysts called for a complete overhaul of the educational system—a comprehensive attempt to rework the basic fabric of schooling, or a restructuring (rebuilding, reinvention, reformation, revolution, rethinking, or transformation) of the educational enterprise.

The purpose of this book is to capture what we have learned to date about restructuring schools. Developing an understanding of the components of restructured schools involves looking in multiple directions. A variety of influential national studies (Boyer, 1983; Goodlad, 1984; Powell et al., 1985; Sizer, 1984) and reports (Carnegie Forum, 1986; Holmes Group, 1986) laid the groundwork for the types of changes needed to develop alternatives to schools as they are currently organized. Thoughtful analysts from organizational theory (Clark & Meloy, 1989; Weick & McDaniel, 1989), political science (Elmore, 1989; Hawley, 1988, 1989), critical theory (Giroux, 1988; Purpel, 1989), teaching and learning (Evertson, Murphy, & Radnofsky, 1990), philosophy and psychology (Adler, 1982; Combs, 1988; Soltis, 1988), and history (D. K. Cohen, 1989; Cuban, 1989; Warren, 1990) have contributed to our understanding about the aspects of schooling most likely to undergo major alterations during a reformation of American public education. A second and third generation of national reports (e.g., Carnegie Council, 1989; Council of Chief State School Officers, 1989; National Governors' Association, 1989; Quality Education for Minorities Project, 1990) have begun to help expand, deepen, and legitimize initial restructuring efforts. Informed advocates for key players likely to be affected by restructuring— whether they be parents (see Seeley, 1980, 1988), teachers (see

Wise, 1989), or students (see Ericson & Ellett, 1989)—are shaping our thinking about the overhaul of the educational system. In addition, respected spokespersons in education (e.g., Bill Honig, Chester Finn, Albert Shanker) and the corporate (e.g., David Kearnes) and political worlds (e.g., Bill Clinton) continue to offer insights into the substance and process of significant educational reform. Important lessons are also beginning to be drawn from those schools, school districts, and states that have begun the difficult process of developing new patterns of management, organization, and delivery of educational services (see David, 1989a; Elmore, 1988a; Moore-Johnson, 1989). Another perspective is provided by analyses of the effects of both current and earlier attempts at decentralizing schooling (see Malen, Ogawa, & Kranz, 1989). Finally, since most of the concepts subsumed under the rubric of reform have a long tradition in education (and in government generally), our knowledge of the components of restructuring is enhanced by tracing key ideas back to their roots.

Looking in multiple directions, or using multiple frames, to understand the phenomenon of restructuring schools enhances the portrait we are able to paint. At one level, the use of multiple perspectives helps guarantee that all the parts are included in the picture. At a second level, it ensures that subtle differences and contrasts are faithfully captured. Finally, it helps make explicit the tensions and rough edges likely to be overlooked when only one or two perspectives are employed.

In chapter 1, I examine the impetus for rebuilding America's schools. I review the classic rationale for decentralized organizations, as well as the more school-specific forces supporting reform. In chapter 2, I provide an overview of restructuring, examining the model that informs the analysis in later chapters and providing an examination of the reasons why the restructured schools movement represents a major change in our thinking about education. In chapters 3–5, I analyze the major components of educational restructuring. Chapter 3 is a treatment of the first of these elements, work redesign. In chapter 4, I examine changes in organization and governance structures. Chapter 5 reviews what is known about restructuring the educational processes, or the core technology, of schools. I begin by presenting ways of understanding changes in educational processes and then review what we have learned about new pedagogy for restructured schools. Chapter 6 is devoted to a critical examination of restructuring and of issues requiring further treatment. I also discuss those factors that will need to be addressed if the seeds of transformational change are likely to flourish.

CHAPTER 1

Impetus for Restructuring Efforts

As with most important changes in the fabric of our social system, the momentum to unfreeze current educational practice and to propel schools toward new forms of governance and management has been supplied by a variety of forces. In this chapter, I examine the underlying pressures for major school reform. Because devolution is at the heart of the reformation movement, I begin by reviewing the classical arguments for organizational decentralization, especially of governmental organizations, that are employed by proponents of restructuring. Then I unpack the complex web of interrelated factors that have supported calls for, and initial experiments with, the comprehensive redesign of the American educational system.

CLASSICAL ARGUMENTS IN SUPPORT OF DECENTRALIZATION

Following the framework developed by Campbell (n.d.), I divide the classical rationale for devolution into political and economic arguments.[1]

Political Theory

The backbone of the political science position on decentralization is "the proposition that the closer government is to the people the more likely it is to be responsive to their demands and interests" (Campbell, n.d., p. 2). Interwoven in this grassroots notion of responsiveness are issues of democracy, constituent influence and control over organizational decisions, ownership of public institutions, trust, and organizational accountability. Proponents of devolution believe that decentralized units increase knowledge about, access to, and participation in governance; make organizations easier to change; and prevent undue consolidation of power at geographically distant locations and hierarchically remote organizational levels. Lurking slightly in the background is the belief that increased responsiveness and accountability will result in more effective and efficient internal operations and the development of a better product or the delivery of a better service.

Restructuring advocates have consistently appealed to the purported political benefits of decentralization in their calls for the transformation of public education.[2] For example, in terms of responsiveness and related issues:

> Proponents of this perspective contend that, by altering influence relationships in these ways, school-based management [SBM] can make schools more successful with their clients, more responsive to their constituencies, more deserving of public support. (Malen et al., 1989, p. 10)

> Greater authority at the school level tends to give rise to more diverse offerings, encourages innovation and responsiveness to community needs, and offers alternatives within the school system. (Carlson, 1989, p. 3)

> Many . . . supporters of radical devolution of power would . . . see the moves towards self-governing schools as a democratic and egalitarian initiative. (Watt, 1989, p. 2)

> In evaluating the overall success of their programs, respondents agreed that principals, staff, parents and students support SBM since they like to be in control of their own destiny. (Clune & White, 1988, p. 25)

> First and foremost is the notion that participation in decision making by a site council representing school constituents will lead to a feeling of ownership by those constituents. This sense of ownership is believed to result in greater acceptance of and cooperation with the implementation of decisions and ultimately produce greater satisfaction for constituents. (Lindquist & Muriel, 1989, p. 405)

The majority of respondents indicated that, with SBM, the school remains more accountable than ever to the district and the state. Respondents indicated that principals were held more accountable as a result of SBM. (Clune & White, 1988, p. 24)

In terms of participation and involvement:

With greater authority and responsibility comes greater accountability. Hence, greater authority will increase the involvement and interest of all with a stake in a school—parents, teachers, principal, and students. And we know that such involvement will benefit the children. (Carlson, 1989, p. 2)

The school community is better informed about school organization and school activities as a result of newsletters sent out by the SBM council. SBM programs have served to increase parents' participation in school decision making, and to increase the community's knowledge of school activities. (Clune & White, 1988, p. 23)

A third rationale for experimenting with new forms of consumer and provider choice is that it may be a way of engaging the creative energy of parents and educators in the solution of serious educational problems, independent of whether choice by itself is a good or effective thing to do. . . . Pushing decisions on finance, staffing, attendance, content, and organization out into the schools may result in more attention at that level to the deliberate design of teaching and learning, rather than to the implementation of plans formulated elsewhere. (Elmore, 1988b, p. 94)

In terms of internal changes in the school:

By giving more authority to, and imposing more responsibility upon teachers and principals, school based management contributes to an overall professionalization of the work force. The committee was told by researchers that effective schools have staffs that share a commitment to excellence and that help one another in moving the school in that direction. (Carlson, 1989, p. 2)

According to Corey, participative management has paid off in commitment from the district's staff: "We have a lot of people out there who not only view themselves as workers in the vineyard but as decision-makers as well. To the degree that their decision-making is real, then, their commitment is real." (Lindelow, 1981, p. 111) of better products and services:

> The major rationale behind SBM is the belief that the closer a deci-
> sion is made to a student served by the decision, the better it is likely
> to serve the student. With adequate authority at the school level,
> many important decisions affecting personnel, curriculum and the
> use of resources can be made by the people who are in the best
> position to make them (those who are most aware of problems and
> needs). (Clune & White, 1988, p. 3)

> We believe that school-based management will result in improve-
> ments in the overall performance of schools, including most impor-
> tantly student achievement. Under a system of school-based man-
> agement, accountability for student achievement rests squarely with
> the individual school. The more that basic decisions affecting stu-
> dents are made at the building level, the greater the likelihood that
> students will be well served. After all, the people most aware of the
> diverse problems and needs in a particular school are those working
> at that level. (Carlson, 1989, p. 2)

Economic Arguments

Proponents of decentralized government organizations maintain that devolution of authority fosters needed competition in
sheltered monopolies. Competition in turn forms the experimen-
tal caldron in which innovations are formed and in which a wide
variety of consumer offerings is produced. As suppliers are forced
to adopt the most effective production techniques, greater efficiency occurs in the expenditure of resources, and organizations
become leaner and more responsive (Bradford, Malt, & Oates,
1969; Maxwell & Aronson, 1977; Oates, 1972). In addition, because
decentralized units are more likely to produce offerings in line
with the differing needs and desires of local groups of citizens,
there is less welfare loss due to collective consumption—or, as
Campbell (n.d.) has noted, "since smaller jurisdictions are likely
to possess more homogeneous populations, it follows that the
package of services provided will more nearly fit their preferences
for public services (p. 4).[3] There is also some evidence to support
advocates' claims that smaller governmental units "may provide
an institutional setting that promotes better decision making by
compelling a more explicit recognition of the costs of public programs" (Oates, 1972, p. 13).

As is the case with those who advance political arguments, we find that proponents of restructured schools have begun to incorporate these economic rationales into their positions.[4] In terms of competition and alternatives:

> When alternatives exist, a material outcome will be more choice among parents and students, as well as a healthy degree of competition among schools. (Carlson, 1989, p. 3)

> Budgeting at the school site, say proponents, increases the efficiency of resource allocation. Teachers and other school staff become more aware of the costs of programs, the school's financial status, and its spending limitations. Old programs "fade away to permit the establishment of alternative new ones, " says Charles W. Fowler [school superintendent]. (Lindelow, 1981, p. 124)

> The major argument in favor of experiments with increased choice is that they provide a much needed prod to a system that is increasingly bureaucratic in its relations with its clients. (Elmore, 1988b, p. 95)

In terms of matching programs with community needs and cost efficiencies:

> It appears that on this basis, decentralizing administration can save up to 2 or 3 percent of a school district's budget. (Carnoy & MacDonell, 1990, p. 58)

> Offsetting the increased costs of SBM are the alleged savings produced from more efficient operations. Schools with school-based budgeting indicated that they spend the same amount of money as other schools, but they spend it more efficiently because they do not waste it on programs and materials they do not need. (Clune & White, 1988, p. 29)

> In Florida, the sixty-seven school districts are county based. Thus, within one county there can be a wide range of communities that have very different educational needs. The weaknesses of centralization come to the fore in systems, such as Florida's, where the diversity within one district can be great. (Lindelow, 1981, p. 101)

> Pierce believes educational efficiency should be defined "in terms of matching available resources with the educational needs of children in schools." Thus, centralized administration, geared to provide uni-

form services, is efficient only if the needs of its clientele are uniform. "If they are different," states Pierce, "then centralized provision may be inefficient." Decentralized administration, on the other hand, is much more capable of matching educational services with the changing needs of students and parents. Its flexible nature allows it to be efficient in the sense that Pierce defines. (Lindelow, 1981, pp. 98–99)

SCHOOL-RELATED FACTORS

The world in which we live is rapidly changing. As we move toward a postindustrial society, a rethinking of the underlying assumptions about our place in this larger world is occurring. Concomitant with this process are attempts to mold organizations to the realities of this new world. Failure to do so, claim the critics, augurs poorly for the long-term well-being of American society. It is within this context that pressures to reinvent schooling are rising. There is a widespread belief that schools must respond to the expanding demands and expectations of society by completely overhauling the way they are organized and governed. Thus a wide array of pressures has combined to force schools to address the question of what they should look like in a postindustrial world. In this section, I examine some of these forces in detail.

Competitive Factors

I believe the success of that second wave of reform is critical, because public education has put this country at a terrible competitive disadvantage. The American workforce is running out of qualified people. (Kearnes, 1988b, p. 566)

As I reported in the Introduction, there is a widely held belief that the failure of the schools to educate youth adequately lies behind America's inability to sustain its "once unchallenged preeminence in commerce, industry, science, and technological innovation" (National Commission on Excellence in Education, 1983, p. 5; see Murphy 1990a, for a review). "In order to sustain our present standard of living and regain our competitive position in the world economy, the argument goes, we will need a better educated workforce" (Elmore, 1989, p. 2). As B. Mitchell (1990, p.

28) has noted, the maxim of "economic salvation through educational excellence" has become widely accepted. Analyses of the problem and demands for improvement have been issued from nearly every sector of society. The prevailing belief that guided early thinking about educational reform in the 1980s was that schools were simply failing to do as good a job of preparing students as they had in the past. Business leaders were particularly vocal in expressing this view (see Kearnes, 1988a, 1988b; Olson, 1990a; Perry, 1988). As I noted in the Introduction, the focus was directed toward repairing the existing system. More recently, reformers have begun to conclude that the model of schooling that was so successful in fueling the industrial economy is simply ill suited to the demands of preparing workers for postindustrial, postbureaucratic organizations (Murphy, 1989b). This conclusion in turn has created pressure on schools to rethink the way they are organized and managed (see Chubb, 1988).[5]

Note how changes in definition of the purpose of schooling and of success parallel the evolution in the needs of the larger society, especially the economy. When businesses required large numbers of semiskilled employees to participate in industrial production, schools were organized to sort students to meet those needs. Given the low level of skills required and a surplus of students (i.e., potential workers), success was relatively easily achieved and, therefore, outcome issues were not of primary concern. As the needs of businesses have changed (from students with basic skills to students who can think, from docile students who could work alone in a crowd to active students who must be able to work cooperatively on nonroutine tasks and who must take ownership of their work), as the level of skills required by workers has risen (from roughly the fourth to ninth grade), and as the number of surplus students has fallen, the economy is demanding not only that schools radically redesign their operations (ideology and core technology) to produce a better product (Seeley, 1980, 1988), but also that they reduce the error rate (B. Mitchell, 1990). Schlechty (1990) states this point nicely in a slightly different way when he notes that "for the first time in the history of humankind, in America at least, education is essential to livelihood" (p. 31). Thus attention to outcomes is much more critical in these restructured schools than it has been historically in education. Note also that the hidden or informal curriculum embedded in the less visible meanings of education's deep message systems, ways of organizing, and interpersonal and structural arrangements—the day-to-day fabric of school and classroom life (see Giroux, 1988)—is also being dramatically altered to become more isomorphic with the evolving conception of corporate cultures.

Demands of a Changing Population

> In sum, the overall condition of children as indicated by income, family structure and background, health, and other measures has changed considerably in the last few years. These changes warrant a reassessment of the delivery services to children and a reconsideration of the appropriate role of the school. (Kirst, McLaughlin, & Massell, 1989, p. 7)

Perhaps for the first time in our history, economic forces and equity issues, or quality and equity values/goals (see Mitchell & Encarnation, 1984; Sergiovanni, Burlingame, Coombs, & Thurston, 1987), are being conjoined (Murphy, 1989b; Seeley, 1988) in the service of improved education for all students. The rapidly changing demographic picture in schools (and in society in general) has been amply documented: schools are increasingly populated by less advantaged youth, children of color, students in need of an array of noneducational services, youngsters from homes where English is not the primary language, and pupils from families in which both parents work or from single-parent homes (Carnegie Council, 1989; Kirst, 1989; Kirst et al., 1989; Quality Education for Minorities Project, 1990; Wagstaff & Gallagher, 1990). These at-risk students, for whom schools have historically been the least successful, will soon constitute fully one third of the student population (Boyd & Hartman, 1988). At the same time, the number of low-skilled jobs in the economy is declining, the demand for highly skilled workers is increasing, and the surplus of workers is falling as the population ages. These conditions are exerting a tremendous force on schools to be more effective for at-risk youth. Given the documented failure of schools as they are currently organized to succeed with these students (see Cuban, 1989; Seeley, 1980), considerable pressure is being applied to restructure education.

Concern with the Standards-Raising Movement

> Much of the rhetoric of the recent education reform movement has been couched in the language of decline, suggesting that standards have slipped, that the education system has grown lax and needs to return to some earlier performance standard to succeed. Our view is very different. We do not believe the educational system needs repairing; we believe it must be rebuilt to match the drastic change needed in our economy if we are to prepare our children for productive lives in the 21st century. (Carnegie Forum, 1986, p. 14)

In the early and mid-1980s, proposals to improve education focused primarily on raising standards by expanding centralized controls. A state-centered, top-down model of change was employed. Prescriptions and performance measurements were emphasized. Piecemeal efforts were undertaken to repair the existing educational system. As I reported in the Introduction, many academics and practitioners found these approaches to be philosophically misguided and conceptually limited (see also Boyd, 1987; Combs, 1988; Deal, 1986; Passow, 1984, 1988). A number of these critics maintained that the standards-raising movement would enhance the site (and district) bureaucracy while diminishing the morale of school site personnel, thereby crippling efforts at real improvement (David, 1989b). Others argued that the standards-raising movement failed to take "into account the most fundamental variables in the educational process: the nature of the relationship between educators and their students and the extent to which students are actively engaged in the learning process" (Sedlak et al., 1986, p. ix).[6] These concerns and criticisms have helped to pave the way for a second phase of educational reform in which a reanalysis of the basic structure of schooling is occurring and the possibility for a "reformation" (Soltis, 1988, p. 243) of American education is being forged.

Disgruntlement with the Bureaucratization of Schools

> The graded public school . . . is an organization that, through no ill intent on the part of the people who work within it, is designed to fail most of the children who have historically been labeled at risk. (Cuban, 1989, p. 783).

> The bureaucratic structure is failing in a manner so critical that adaptations will not forestall its collapse. (Clark & Meloy, 1989, p. 293)

All of the school-based pressures for the restructuring of education lead back to concerns with the prevailing model of governance, organization, program delivery, and management of schools. In short, the bureaucratic infrastructure of schools has come under severe criticism[7] from (1) those who argue that schools are so covered with bureaucratic sediment that initiative, creativity, and professional judgment have all been paralyzed (Bolin, 1989; Chubb & Moe, 1990; Conley, 1989; Frymier, 1987) and the likely success of reforms has been neutralized (Chubb, 1988; Lomotey & Swanson, 1990; Sizer, 1984); (2) critics who maintain that "bureaucratic management practices have been causing unacceptable distortions in educational process" (Wise, 1989, p. 301), that they are "paralyzing American education . . . [and] getting in the way of children's learning" (Sizer, 1984, p. 206; also Cuban, 1989; McNeil, 1988a, 1988b, 1988c; Wise 1978, 1988); (3) analysts who believe that bureaucracy is counterproductive to the needs and interests of educators within the school—"that it is impractical, and it does not fit the psychological and personal needs of the workforce" (Clark & Meloy, 1989, p. 293; see also Bolin, 1989; Frymier, 1987); (4) critics who suggest that bureaucratic management is inconsistent with the sacred values and purposes of education—who question "fundamental ideological issues pertaining to bureaucracy's meaning in a democratic society" (Campbell et al., 1987, p. 73; see American Association of Colleges of Teacher Education, 1988; Angus, 1988; Giroux, 1988; National Center for Effective Schools Research and Development, 1989); (5) scholars who view bureaucracy as a form of operation that inherently forces attention away from the core technology of schooling—

> Since the student is the prime producer of learning and since he is not part of the bureaucracy, and not subject to bureaucratic accountability, bureaucracy and its whole value structure must be seen as irrelevant at best, and obstructive at worst, to true learning relationships. (Seeley, 1980, p. 8);

(6) reform proponents who hold that the existing organizational structure of schools is neither sufficiently flexible nor sufficiently

robust to meet the needs of students in a technoservice (Maccoby, 1988) or postindustrial society (Beare, 1989; Harvey & Crandall, 1988; Sizer, 1984); and (7) analysts who believe that the rigidities of bureaucracy impede the ability of parents and citizens to govern and reform schooling (see Campbell et al., 1987). This tremendous attack on the bureaucratic infrastructure of schools has led to demands to develop alternative methods of operating that are grounded on new values and principles:

> Our analysis suggests that people who create organizational designs for schools should construct forms that aid the articulation and development of professional values, since these values are sources of guidance when people process nonroutine information. Our review also suggests that organic organizational forms are better designs both for developing values and for clarifying vague causal structures than are mechanistic forms. Since organic forms also encourage the development of substitutes for leadership, they encourage professional development as well as utilize current skills and attitudes. (Weick & McDaniel, 1989, p. 350; see also Clark & Meloy, 1989; Combs, 1988; Wise, 1989)

Crisis in the Teaching Force

> Still another motive for restructuring schools arises from what many perceive to be an emerging crisis of quality in the teaching force. A large proportion of the current teaching force will leave through attrition or retirement in the next decade. This teacher turnover will occur during a period of broad changes in the labor force. Education is losing its claim on the labor pool from which teachers have traditionally been drawn—who now have access to other professional occupations. If education is to regain its competitive position in the labor market, the argument goes, schools will have to be more attractive places to work and the economic rewards of teaching will have to be competitive with other professional occupations. (Elmore, 1989, pp. 2–3)

A documented crisis in the teaching force has led to nearly universal calls for the professionalization of teaching and the organizations in which they work, for a restructuring of schools to develop the type of work environment that empowers teachers and promotes continuous professional development. Proponents of restructuring maintain that organizations with strong professional cultures, where there is "access to frequent collegial interaction about complex problems of practice, access to the knowledge required to enhance professional development, differential rewards for people who develop knowledge and skill at a significantly higher level than their colleagues, and access to the basic resources necessary to good performance" (Elmore, 1988a, p. 1), are required if education is to be able to attract and keep a quality labor force (see Boyer, 1983; Carnegie Forum, 1986; Goodlad, 1984; Holmes Group, 1986; Sizer, 1984; Wise, 1989). The correlation between professionalism and restructuring has been succinctly stated by the Holmes Group (1986) in their report on *Tomorrow's Teachers:* "If the construction of a genuine profession of teaching is to succeed, schools will have to change" (p. 67). Wise (1989) reinforces the need to move in this direction when he concludes that "the professionalization of teaching is as much about the preservation of the public school tradition as anything else" (p. 309) (see also Thompson, 1988). Thus we find calls for greater professionalism joining forces with demands for less bureaucracy. Both are pushing reformers to radically revise traditional mechanistic organizational structures in favor of systems of governance more compatible with organic forms of organization (see Clark & Meloy, 1989; Weick & McDaniel, 1989).

School Effectiveness and School Improvement Research

> There is little point in concluding that our schools are in trouble and then focusing for improvement only on teachers or principals, or the curriculum. All of these and more are involved. Consequently, efforts at improvement must encompass the school as a system of interacting parts, each affecting the others. (p. 31)

> The guiding principle being put forward here is that the school must become largely self-directing. (Goodlad, 1984, p. 276)

School effectiveness and school improvement research have contributed a good deal of both support and pressure for transforming school systems (Bredeson, 1989; Clune & White, 1988; Murphy, 1990c, 1990d). Two of the major findings from these complementary lines of research (see Clark, Lotto, & Astuto, 1984, for a review) are that school improvement is an integrated rather than a piecemeal activity and that improvement occurs on a school-by-school basis. In building on these conclusions, it has been argued that each school should be provided with substantial autonomy and should become "the fundamental decision making unit within the educational system" (Guthrie, 1986, p. 306).[8] As Chubb (1988) has reported:

> The more control a school has over those aspects of its organization that affect its performance—the articulation of goals, the selection and management of teachers, the specification of policies—the more likely it is to exhibit the qualities that have been found to promote effectiveness. (p. 37)

Proposals for the devolution of control are at the heart of efforts to restructure schools. Endorsed by a number of major reform reports (e.g., the National Commission on Excellence in Educational Administration, 1987), this organizational arrangement represents a radical shift from the status quo in school governance and management.

Lessons from the Corporate World

> The changes all point to the fact that the new kind of educational organizational structure is intended to be both post-bureaucratic and post-industrial. As has happened so often in the past, education is being forced to adopt the modes of organization which appear to be successful in the business or private sector. (Beare, 1989, p. 14)

Advocates for school restructuring have found support for fundamentally different methods of operation from modern management theory and from activities in the corporate sector (Association for Supervision and Curriculum Development, 1986; Schlechty, 1990; Thompson, 1988). Faced with a series of problems not unlike those confronting schools—diminished product quality, low employee morale, unhappy consumers—businesses looked inward to see how the most successful of their group were operating (see Deal & Kennedy, 1982; Peters & Waterman, 1982). By and large, it was discovered that the most effective corporations had transformed their businesses by decentralizing operations—by pushing decisions down to the level of the organization in closest contact with the customer, by reorienting their management philosophy from control to empowerment, by establishing scrupulous reputations for attention to quality, and by changing their views of workers—from property of the company to partners in the corporate undertaking (Beare, 1989; Maccoby, 1989; Peters & Waterman, 1982). In short, they had restructured themselves from more hierarchically organized units to more fluid and organic systems.[9] These lessons are now being held up to schools, especially by corporate managers (see Kearnes, 1988a, 1988b), as blueprints for educational reform. There is considerable pressure on educators to adopt these blueprints and transform school operations consistent with the organizational revolution occurring in the private sector.

SUMMARY

What is clear for schooling in the United States is that the environment is heating up. There is less certainty and more turbulence in the air as society undertakes a thorough reexamination of the most appropriate form for education in the postindustrial world (Malen et al., 1989). Schools have been forced to respond. For a variety of reasons reported herein—systemic concerns about the vitality of the American economy, disgruntlement with the mechanistic model of schooling and dissatisfaction with efforts to reform schools based on that model, the crisis in the teaching profession, lessons gleaned from successful educational and corporate enterprises—there has been a shift away from schooling as a production- and efficiency-driven system toward a market-sensitive system. The mass production perspective of the past is giving way, grudgingly, to more customized technologies. Mechanistic forms of management and control are beginning to be replaced by more organic forms of organization. These restructured schools, in their incipient stages of development, are characterized by greater decentralization, a higher degree of internal differentiation, and more autonomous work units. There is less rigidity to internal structures, responsibilities are less firmly anchored to specific roles, and control and coordination have less to do with hierarchical authority than with cooperative work efforts. In the next five chapters, I examine the elements of these restructured schools in more detail.

CHAPTER 2

Restructuring: An Overview

In this chapter, I provide an overview of what follows in chapters 3–5. I do this in two ways. First, I present the conceptual framework that undergirds this later work. Second, I analyze the significance of the elements that comprise this framework. I reveal how restructuring has the potential to radically alter the way that schools are run and that students learn.

APPROACHES TO RESTRUCTURING

As I discuss more thoroughly in chapters 3 through 5, restructuring generally encompasses systemic changes in one or more of the following: work roles and organizational milieu; organizational and governance structures, including connections among the school and its larger environment; and core technology. Restructuring also involves fundamental alterations in the relationships among the players involved in the educational process. Figure 2.1 provides a picture of these changes in organizational elements and relationships. This framework guides my treatment of restructuring throughout this volume. In this chapter, my goal is simply to outline the key parts of the model.[1] The rectangles represent the key *actors*: state officials, superintendent, principal, parents, teachers, and students. The lines connecting the various players are designed to explicate some of the predominant *components* of restructuring: changes in the design of work, alterations in organization and governance structures, and revisions to the core technology. The circles—school-based management (SBM), choice, teacher empowerment, and teaching for understanding—represent the four most prevalent *strategies* employed in restructuring schools. The italicized phrases, e.g., teachers as leaders, parents as partners, are the new *metaphors* of restructuring. For purposes of organization, I have developed my chapters around

15

Figure 2.1. Restructuring schools: A conceptual framework.

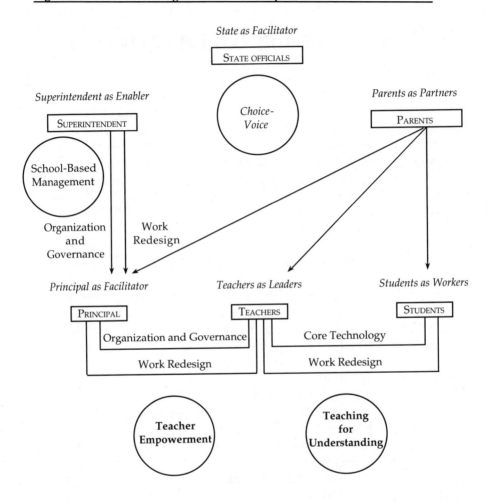

the three *components* of restructuring. Discussions of *actors, strategies,* and *metaphors* are subsumed under that dimension of the framework.

Even a cursory review of the framework in Figure 2.1 shows the complexity involved in transforming schooling. It should also be obvious that restructuring efforts can begin in a variety of places and employ a number of different strategies depending upon the specific objectives sought. The framework is also designed to convey the message that real educational transformation will require the involvement of all the key players, work on all components of the system, and the simultaneous use of four distinct but interrelated restructuring strategies. To date, most efforts at reformation have emphasized only one or two strategies. Teacher empowerment held center stage at the outset of the restructuring movement. More recently, attention has shifted to school-based management and choice. Considerably less work has been devoted to teaching for understanding, or redefining the teaching–learning process, although the rumblings of early movements in this area are becoming distinctly audible.

SIGNIFICANCE OF RESTRUCTURING

A number of important changes embedded in our attempts to reinvent schooling augur fundamental shifts in our view of education.[2] The potential to dramatically alter our understanding of schooling is woven throughout transformation efforts embedded in the framework in Figure 2.1. To begin with, restructuring encompasses a basic change in our view of the relationship between the school and its environment. Historically ingrained notions of schools as sheltered monopolies, or delivery systems, are breaking down under the incursions of a market philosophy into education (see Boyd, 1990; Boyd & Hartman, 1988). The traditional dominant relationship between schools (and professional educators) and the public is being reworked in favor of more nearly equal arrangements, i.e., partnerships (Seeley, 1980, 1988). For the first time in our history, the business of schooling is being redefined in relation to the customer. Restructuring is facilitating unprecedented inroads of market forces into the governance and organization of schools (see Chubb & Moe, 1990). It is also fostering "significant changes in the way that states relate to schools" (El-more, 1988a, p. 2; see also David, Cohen, Honetschlager, & Trai-man, 1990; Le Tendre, 1990).

Consistent with this change are efforts to develop new forms of school organization and management. The basic organizing and management principle of schooling—knowledge of loss (see Mitchell, 1990)—is giving way to more proactive attempts to govern educational systems. In addition, a new "social physics" (Bell, cited in Campbell et al., 1987, p. 26) that promises to significantly change the nature of social relationships in schools is emerging. The hierarchical, bureaucratic organizational structures that have defined schools over the past 80 years are giving way to more decentralized (Guthrie, 1986; M. J. Murphy & Hart, 1988) and more professionally controlled systems (David, 1989a; Houston, 1989)—systems that "can be thought of as a new paradigm for school management" (Wise, 1989, p. 303). In these new postindustrial organizations (see Beare, 1989), labeled heterarchies by Maccoby (1989), there are "very basic changes in roles, relationships, and responsibilities" (Seeley, 1988, p. 35): traditional patterns of relationships are altered (Conley, 1989; Rallis, 1990), authority flows are less hierarchical (Clark & Meloy, 1989), role definitions are both more general and more flexible (Corcoran, 1989), leadership is connected to competence for needed tasks rather than to formal position (American Association of Colleges of Teacher Education, 1988; Angus, 1988; Maccoby 1988, 1989), and independence and isolation are replaced by cooperative work (Beare, 1989). Furthermore, a traditional structural orientation[3] is being overshadowed by a focus on the human element. The operant goal is no longer maintenance of the organizational infrastructure but rather the development of human resources (Mojkowski & Fleming, 1988; Schlechty, 1990). Developing learning climates and organizational adaptivity are being substituted for the more traditional emphasis on uncovering and applying the one best model of performance (Clark & Meloy, 1989; McCarthey & Peterson, 1989). The changed metaphors being applied to these restructured schools—e.g., from principal as manager to principal as facilitator, from teacher as worker to teacher as leader—nicely portray these fundamental revisions in our understanding of social relationships and in our views of organizations and conceptions of management. They reveal a reorientation in transformed schools from control to empowerment.

At the same time, some very early initiatives are underway that suggest that we may be on the threshold of major changes throughout the teaching–learning process. A more robust understanding of the educational production function has begun to be translated into "dramatically different way[s] of thinking about the design, delivery, and documentation of instructional programs" (Spady, 1988, p. 8). The strongest theoretical or disciplinary influence on education—psychology—is being pushed off center stage by newer sociological perspectives. Underlying these changes are radically different ways of thinking about the "educability of humanity" (Purpel, 1989, p. 10; see also Oakes & Lipton, 1990). Schools that were historically organized to produce results consistent with the normal curve, to sort youth into the various strata needed to fuel the economy, are being redesigned to ensure equal opportunity and success for all learners (see Miller & Brookover, 1986).[4] Seeley (1988) astutely notes the importance of this change when he comments that "it represents a significant shift in the goals of our educational system, and a fundamental component of a new vision, since all other components gain motive force from this shift in goals" (p. 34).

At the center of these changes in social ecology is a not so subtle shift in assumptions about knowledge. As Fisher (1990) correctly notes, the alpha paradigm of knowledge—the view that "knowledge can be assumed to be an external entity existing independently of human thought and action, and hence, something about which one can be objective" (p. 82)—"dominant for so long in classroom practice, has begun to be critically examined in a new way" (p. 84). A new view, one that holds that knowledge is internal and subjective, that it "depends on the values of the persons working with it and the context within which that work is conducted" (p. 82), is receiving serious consideration. Knowledge is personal and contextualized. Learning is a social phenomenon. New views about what is worth learning are emerging in restructuring schools. In these classrooms, the traditional emphasis on content coverage and rote learning of basic skills is being challenged by more in-depth treatment of topics and a focus on higher order thinking skills (Carnegie Council, 1989). Educators are beginning to acknowledge "that thinking is secondary to acting" (Dokecki, 1990, p. 160). Attention has been turned to active learning, and a century-old concern for independent work and competition—a focus on the individual dimension of human existence—is slowly receding in favor of more cooperative learning relationships—a focus on the social dimensions of human existence (David, 1989a). Equally important, a long-standing concern with the technical dimensions of teaching and learning is giving way to a renewed emphasis on the need to personalize schooling. Or, as Dokecki (1990) has nicely stated, the "centrality of caring has been recognized recently by a number of professional fields" (p. 163) and caring is beginning to be seen as the "regulative ideal" of intervention in these professions.[5]

"An elevated conceptualization of teaching" (Rallis, 1990, p. 193) consistent with the epistemological change noted above is embedded in restructuring schools. The importance of craft knowledge is explicitly recognized for the first time since the onslaught of scientific management. Rather than seek ways to simplify instruction, the complexity of teaching is acknowledged and nurtured (Petrie, 1990). Teachers are allotted considerable discretion over pedagogy. The teacher-centered instruction that is at the heart of the factory model of classroom instruction is giving way to growing demands for a learner-centered pedagogy. The model of the teacher as a "sage on a stage" (Fisher, 1990, p. 83), in which instructors are viewed as content specialists who possess the relevant knowledge that they transmit to students through telling, is replaced by an approach in which "teaching is more like coaching, where the student (as opposed to the teacher) is the primary performer" (p. 83; see also Sizer, 1984). In this revised approach, teachers act as facilitators (McCarthey & Peterson, 1989), modelers (Spady, 1988), and coaches (Sizer, 1984) who invest "students with increased power and responsibility for their own learning" (Elmore, 1988a, p. 3). The emphasis in restructured schools is on the student rather than on the deliverer. Students are seen as "producers of knowledge" and teachers "as managers of learning experiences" (Hawley, 1989, p. 32). The focus is on learning, not on the delivery system (Seeley, 1980).

Underlying all these changes is an evolution in sacred educational values (see Corbett, Firestone, & Rossman, 1987; Lortie, 1975) and approaches to improvement (see Murphy, 1989a, for an analysis). Alterations in roles and responsibilities are being accompanied by changes in beliefs and values, and holistic, global, and comprehensive reform efforts are replacing the earlier "wave[s] of discrete programs and approaches" (David, 1989a, p.

45; see also Lindquist & Muriel, 1989; Seeley, 1988). For example, discussions about the purpose of schooling have been reopened (Elmore, 1988a) as the needs of the economy have changed. Teacher egalitarianism and isolation are beginning to crack under the new organizational imperatives for differentiated roles and collegial work. The reward structure for professionals is being fundamentally altered. Teachers who historically derived almost all their rewards from interactions with their students (see Lortie, 1975) are becoming more dependent on colleagues' judgments about the quality of their performance. The historically conservative fabric of teaching is being rewoven in many places with bold initiatives—both in individual schools and districts and in the profession as a whole. And perhaps most dramatically of all, success is no longer defined primarily in terms of providing services (processes) but rather in terms of product quality (outcomes) (Bolin, 1989; M. J. Murphy & Hart, 1988).[6] Consistent with this last change, there is renewed interest in educational equity—examining outcomes for all children. There has also been a dramatic rethinking about accountability for results (Murphy, 1989c). As Cuban (1989) has aptly reported, there has been a radical shift in responsibility for low achievement from the student and the family to the school.

SUMMARY

In this chapter, I laid the groundwork for the analysis to follow. I examined the conceptual framework (in Figure 2.1) that shapes the way I unpack the restructuring phenomenon for inspection in later chapters. I also discussed how the elements of that framework—the strategies, components, and metaphors—represent a significantly different perspective about the entire schooling process. Using the components of this framework—work redesign, organizational and governance structures, and core technology—as my organizing format, I now turn my attention to an in-depth analysis of restructuring.

CHAPTER 3

Work Redesign

*When you create a center of inquiry, then different roles
and relationships will ensue. (Goodlad, cited in Bradley,
1989, November 1, p. 12)*

One of the key ingredients of school restructuring is a redefinition of the roles and responsibilities of professional staff. As outlined in Figure 2.1, this includes the redesign of work relationships between the superintendent (district office) and the principal (school) and between the principal and the teachers. In general, restructuring work signals

> a major shift in how people in school systems think about roles and relationships. The shift is from a system characterized by controlling and directing what goes on at the next lower level to guiding and facilitating professionals in their quest for more productive learning opportunities for students. (David, 1989a, p. 28)

Reform also involves changes in the bureaucratic principle of specialization of labor. In postindustrial organizations, there is reduced emphasis on dividing responsibilities into an ever-increasing number of discrete roles:

> Specialization is no longer seen as a strength. There is increasing emphasis on generalist (rather than specialist) skills; the new organization requires adaptable people who can turn their hands to several tasks and who view the organizational and professional world more globally than the narrow specialist. (Beare, 1989, p. 15)

This principle of work redesign applied to schools has been nicely described by one of the prime forces in transforming education, the Coalition of Essential Schools:

> The principal and teachers should perceive themselves as generalists first (teachers and scholars in general education) and specialists

second (experts in but one particular discipline). Staff should expect multiple obligations (teacher-counselor-manager) and a sense of commitment to the entire school. (Houston, 1989, p. 6)

In practical terms, for schools in the process of restructuring, this means more emphasis on interdependence and cooperative work teams that trade assignments and provide opportunities for teachers and administrators to confront a variety of problems with a variety of professional colleagues (Clark & Meloy, 1989). It means viewing teaching as "an uncommon mix of many tasks" (Cuban, 1989, p. 800). A corollary of this idea is that responsibilities in redesigned schools are less role dependent. The historically ingrained distinctions between teachers and administrators begin to blur (Giroux, 1988; Petrie, 1990). Functions are more likely to gravitate to actors with technical competence rather than to be assigned to specific roles. In a similar vein, leadership is decoupled from authority attached to specific roles (Sergiovanni, 1989; Sykes & Elmore, 1989); it is more closely connected than it has been historically to professional expertise (Angus, 1988). Let us direct our attention now to an analysis of how work is altered for each of the professional actors in restructured schools.

DISTRICT OFFICE

If restructuring schools means changing the conditions of teaching and learning, it also means taking up the challenge of changing the conditions of leadership. The metaphors of steward, captain, visionary, evangelist, manager, or instructional leader are inadequate because they suggest leadership is confined to a role or described by a set of skills or tasks to be accomplished. (Rallis, 1990, p. 203)

The central office must come to see itself not as a regulator or initiator, but as a service provider. The primary function of the central office must be to assure that individual schools have what they need to be successful. (Carlson, 1989, p. 3)

If schools are to be transformed, it is clear that the role of the central office will need to change, especially the prevailing view of the superintendency (Clune & White, 1988; National Commission on Excellence in Educational Administration, 1987). In fact, "the relationship that will be most changed by the implementation of school-based management is that between the central office and school site" (Lindelow, 1981, p. 116). Although the roles of school board members themselves will be little altered in restructured schools, their views about the functions of administrators and teachers may require significant change (Lindelow, 1981). In short, board members will need to be in agreement philosophically with the tenets of restructuring if parents and school staffs are to have a chance to successfully rethink the pedagogy and the organization and management of schools (Finn & Clements, 1989).

The work of superintendents and their staffs, on the other hand, changes dramatically in restructured school systems (Harrison, Killion, & Mitchell, 1989). As the new metaphor for the superintendency in Figure 2.1 reveals, the chief executive officers of reformed schools act, not as they traditionally have, as directors and controllers, but as coordinators and "enablers" (Bradley, 1989, November 1, p. 12)—their job "is to facilitate, not dictate" (Lindelow, 1981, p. 112). One of their main functions is "serving and assisting schools" (Chapman & Boyd, 1986, p. 34; see also Bradley, 1989, November 1). In this role, central offices act as service providers (Carlson, 1989) or support centers (Fernandez, 1989) that offer technical assistance to schools (Clune & White, 1988; David, 1989b). Under this new type of work design, schools can contract with the district office for services as needed or desired (Thompson, 1988). The key element here is that schools have the freedom to engage district resources or not (Harrison et al., 1989).[1] In their role of enabler, district personnel also need to "build the capacity of schools to take advantage of the opportunities of decentralization" (J. T. Murphy, 1989, p. 811). District offices maintain their responsibility for establishing the overall direction for the enterprise and for measuring the success of each school's programs (Lindelow, 1981). However, in a transformed school system, they undertake these functions, not by appeal to "centrally enforced rule," but by "management by exception" (J. T. Murphy, 1989, p. 811). Thus, they focus their energy on those parts of the organization experiencing difficulty.

The redesign of work responsibilities outlined above has important implications both for the structure of district operations and for the definition of the superintendency itself (David, 1989b; Elmore, 1988a; Moore-Johnson, 1989). Central offices often become considerably smaller in restructured school districts. For example, one of the first restructuring acts of New York City School Chancellor Fernandez was to eliminate 218 central office positions (Bradley, 1990, January 17). The remaining organization is often flatter, less hierarchical (Bradley, 1989, October 18; Chapman & Boyd, 1986; David, 1989a; Sickler, 1988). As this leveling of the organizational pyramid occurs, responsibilities historically undertaken (and personnel historically housed) at the district level are transferred to schools (Lindelow, 1981) and "functions that are currently centralized will be spread over a larger number of people" (Thompson, 1988, p. 15). The role of the remaining "middle managers becomes more focused on providing services directly to schools" (David, 1989a, p. 29). Salaries are sometimes realigned to place principals at the top of the administrative pay scale (Guthrie, 1986; Kearnes, 1988a). Finally, the definition of the superintendency in restructured schools also appears ripe for change. As J. T. Murphy (1989) has astutely noted, in decentralized schools

> we need to shift our thinking about what it means to be a strong superintendent. We need to develop some gentler, more feminine images of leadership to accompany our tough, masculine images of leadership . . . superintendents need to pay more attention to the unheroic dimensions of leadership if they are to promote local autonomy and professionalism. Superintendents must not only have personal vision, but they must also work with others to develop a shared vision and to find the common ground; they must not only have answers, but also ask the right questions; they must not only persuade, but also listen carefully and consult widely before making decisions; they must not only wield power, but also depend on others and develop caring relationships; they must not only exercise leadership, but also nurture the development of leadership throughout the school district. In this view, the real heroes are not the highly visible superintendents at the top but the less visible professionals and parents throughout the system who work directly with students. (p. 810)

PRINCIPAL

We argue that the deregulating and accountability reforms being envisioned will dramatically alter the work and role expectations of building administrators. (M. J. Murphy & Hart, 1988, pp. 1–2)

That is, empowering teachers will also expand and change the responsibilities of the principal. (Thompson, 1988, p. 10)

If the relationship between the district office and the school is
the key element of change in the school-based management strategy, the relationship that is most changed in the teacher empowerment strategy is that between the principal and the teachers.
Thus, in many ways, the principal is the nexus of restructuring
efforts—accepting additional autonomy and accountability on be-
half of the school and passing it through to the teaching staff (and
to the larger community).

There is, however, palpable tension between the role envisioned for the principal by those who attempt to transform
schools through site-based management and those who rely on a
strategy of teacher empowerment—a tension that often leaves
principals confused about what is expected of them and feeling
"left out on a limb" (Chapman & Boyd, 1986, p. 30).[2] In the former
strategy, "the principal becomes the central actor" (Lindelow,
1981, p. 116). The role changes from "dependent business manager to autonomous educational leader" (Clune & White, 1988, p.
7; see Murphy, 1990d, for a review). In an empowerment model
(whether of teachers or parents or both), the principal retains an
important role but not the one of greatest centrality. Neither is he
or she an autonomous educational leader. Rather, the principal
acts as a coordinator of a group of professionals: "The principal
now becomes relocated from the apex of the pyramid to the center
of the network of human relationships and functions as a change
agent and resource" (Chapman & Boyd, 1986, p. 55). Administration becomes "a support function for teaching rather than a mech-
anism for the control of teaching" (Bolin, 1989, p. 88; Moore-
Johnson, 1989). This latter view of the principalship is much softer
and much less directive than the former.

In either case, however, restructuring will necessitate major
changes in the roles and responsibilities of building administrators. It is perhaps best to think of the principal's role as changing
from "that of a middle manager for the district" (Lindelow, 1981,
p. 128) to that of facilitator-leader for his or her school (Bradley,
1989, November 1; see also Carnoy & MacDonell, 1990):

The new manager . . . will not be a classical, hierarchically oriented
bureaucrat but a customized version of Indiana Jones: proactive, en-

trepreneurial, communicating in various languages, able to inspire, motivate and persuade subordinates, superiors, colleagues and outside constituents. (Gerding and Serenhuijseur, cited in Beare, 1989, p. 19)

It is becoming increasingly clear that this change will make the principal's job not only more exciting but also more complex and more demanding; new responsibilities are being added, but "few if any of the former role demands [are being] taken away" (Bredeson, 1989, p. 16). In general, it appears that principals in restructured schools will need to place considerably more emphasis on three areas of responsibility—technical core operations, people management, and school–environmental relations. To begin with, because "one of the immediate results of decentralization and devolution [is] to put great pressures on the principal as curriculum leader" (Chapman & Boyd, 1986, p. 42), principals will "have to attend to a much larger set of managerial tasks tied to the delivery of educational services" (Lindelow, 1981, p. 120) than they have done historically.[3] Principals will also move "closer to the staff as mediator[s] of shared governance" (Clune & White, 1988, p. 19). This shift dramatically highlights the importance of participatory leadership and administrators' interpersonal communication skills (Bradley, 1989, November 1; Bredeson, 1989; Schlechty, 1990). It also underscores the need for principals to develop a better understanding of adult development and learning and of strategies and techniques for working with adults (Murphy, in press; Rallis, 1990). Finally, there is evidence that establishing and nurturing relationships with the larger environment will require more administrative time. In restructured schools, principals "assume a more public role, interacting with people in the wider community, [and] forging links between the school and the environment" (Chapman & Boyd, 1986, p. 48). Thus it appears that principals will need to concentrate more energy and effort in their boundary-spanning role, both between the school and the district office (Clune & White, 1988) and between the school and the larger environment (Bredeson, 1989; Fernandez, 1989).

TEACHERS

The solution is to empower teachers, to help them develop an internalized locus of control. (Frymier, 1987, p. 14)

The consortium . . . wishes to see nothing less than the transformation of teaching from an occupation into a genuine profession.
(Holmes Group, 1986, p. ix)

Structural Roles and Responsibilities

Reformers concerned with teacher empowerment envision
comprehensive changes in the work performed by teachers in restructured schools.[4] In fact, a number of authors maintain that
"the development of new leadership roles for teachers [is] on the
crest of the wave" of restructuring (Smylie & Denny, 1989, p. 2).
For purposes of analysis, I divide these changes into three categories: expanded responsibilities, new professional roles, and
new career opportunities (see Figure 3.1). While these groupings
represent important gradations in the opportunities that teachers
have to participate in their schools, all three are characterized by
a dispersal of authority and leadership (M. J. Murphy & Hart,
1988) and by enlarged "teachers' roles and responsibilities beyond
their regular classroom assignments" (Smylie & Denny, 1989,
p. 4).

The redesign of teacher work is based on a number of important premises. One is that teaching is a moral activity and as such
should be subject to the control of teachers themselves (Angus,
1988; Bolin, 1989). A second is that teachers are intellectuals and
should, therefore, take the lead role in discussions about the nature and purposes of schooling (Giroux, 1988). A related argument is grounded on the professional dimensions of teaching
(Petrie, 1990). According to reformers who tackle restructuring
from this base, teaching is a profession and as such should be
guided by professional canons rather than by bureaucratic rules
and regulations (Carnegie Forum, 1986; Clark & Meloy, 1989;
Wise, 1989). Supporting lines of analysis are derived from organizational theorists who conclude that the single leadership model
based on line authority and role position is dysfunctional (Clark &
Meloy, 1989; Maccoby, 1988; Murphy, 1988). Reformers in this
camp maintain that we should think of leadership in terms of its
density in the organization (Sergiovanni, 1989)—that schools
should "ensure that a much larger number of members of the organization are capable of taking on pieces of the leadership role"
(Clinton, 1987, p. 12), and that "leadership roles are shared and

Figure 3.1 Redesign of teacher work

NEW ROLES, STRUCTURAL	NEW ROLES, CONCEPTUAL
Expanded responsibilities	colleague
	decision
New professional roles	leader
	learner
New career opportunities	generalist

PROFESSIONAL ORGANIZATIONAL CULTURE
- enhanced occupational conditions of teaching
- teacher autonomy and control
- collegial interaction
- professional growth

leadership broadly exercised" (Sergiovanni, 1989, p. 221). They also hold that leadership and authority are separate constructs (Heifetz, 1988; Murphy, Hallinger, & Mitman, 1983) and that leadership is better connected to expertise than to line authority (American Association of Colleges for Teacher Education, 1988; Heifetz, 1988).

Expanded responsibilities.   At one level, teachers in schools that are restructuring are taking on new responsibilities. They are assuming control over decisions that were historically the province of others, especially administrators. Changes in this area are of two types—"those that increase teachers' right to participate in formal decision making [and] those that give teachers greater access to influence by making school structures more flexible" (Moore-Johnson, 1989, p. 2). Numerous examples of expanded teacher responsibilities are available from school districts that are engaged in fundamental reform efforts (see Casner-Lotto, 1988; David, 1989a).[5]

Team approaches to school management and governance (see Hallinger & Richardson, 1988) are particularly good collective examples of expanded responsibilities for teachers. For example, in the restructured Cincinnati school system, an equal number of teachers and administrators now comprise the committee that determines the allocation of teachers to individual schools (Moore-

Johnson, 1988). The formalization of teacher participation in decision-making forums from which they were previously excluded (e.g., principal and teacher selection committees, facility planning groups) has been accomplished in Dade County, Florida (Fernandez, 1989), Hammond, Indiana (Casner-Lotto, 1988), and other districts employing school-based models of management (Lindelow, 1981; Olson, 1988). Through expanded participation in collective decision-making models and professional support groups, teachers in restructuring schools have also begun to exercise considerable influence over the type of evaluation procedures employed—"setting standards for their own performance" (Dade County, 1989, p. 13). Individual teachers are often assuming greater responsibility for the mentoring and supervision of their peers—especially beginning teachers—evaluating the work of principals, providing professional development to their colleagues, and developing curricula for the school (Career-ladder, 1990; Corcoran, 1989; McCarthey & Peterson, 1989; Moore-Johnson, 1988, 1989; Sickler, 1988; see David, 1989a, for a review). In short, both individually and collectively, teachers in restructured schools are accumulating new responsibilities that extend their role beyond the confines of their own classrooms.

New professional roles. Some teachers in transformed schools are not only adding new responsibilities to their current jobs but are also beginning to fill new professional roles. The difference between this category and the former one is a matter of extent. In examining expanded responsibilities, I was primarily concerned with new functions that are added to existing role definitions. Here I am more interested in work redesign activities that may significantly alter the basic role itself. For example, a master teacher may continue to work three or four days a week in his or her own classroom but may also spend one or two days working with colleagues in their classrooms or with peers developing student assessment materials. A teacher-facilitator or coordinator may actually leave the classroom for a semester or a year to create professional development activities or curriculum materials for peers. In almost all these cases, however—as opposed to new career lines—role changes are not permanent. Most of the new roles assumed by teacher-facilitators or mentor-teachers will be shed after a period of time, and they will then return to full-time instructional work with students (see Fernandez, 1989; Moore-Johnson, 1988, for other examples of new roles).

New career opportunities. Work redesign for teachers in restructured schools also includes the development of more permanent career opportunities that create the chance "for gifted, well-prepared educators to move upward in their chosen profession without leaving the classroom" (Goodlad, 1984, p. 301). A differentiated staffing arrangement—like the four-step career-ladder model (intern, resident, professional, lead teacher) in Rochester and Cincinnati and the ladder plans in Tennessee, Kentucky, and Utah—is the most well-employed strategy of restructuring work to create new career lines for teachers (see Bradley, 1989, October 18; David, 1989a; Fernandez, 1989; Malen & Hart, 1987). New career roles that are not sequentially packaged, like lead teachers and teacher-directors in Dade County, Florida, and District 4 in New York, are also beginning to be developed:

> Lead Teachers, Teacher-Directors, and Teacher-Coordinators are a growing part of the Dade County landscape. In the county's Satellite Learning Centers, schools at the workplace, Lead Teachers now supervise the program's operation in cooperation with their host school's principal. Lead Teachers teach classes; but they also perform appropriate administrative/supervisory duties on a day-to-day basis, while remaining part of the teachers' bargaining unit. A new position of Teacher-Coordinator has been established for programs of districtwide scope. The first Teacher-Coordinator is supervising the Future Educators of America chapter program. . . . Also remaining part of the teachers' bargaining unit are Teacher-Directors. They assume even more responsibility than do Lead Teachers by working under a county level administrator, and being exclusively responsible for the programs they direct, including the Teacher Education Center and the Dade Academy for the Teaching Arts. (Dade County, 1989, p. 11)

Conceptual Roles

Although the categorization outlined above—responsibilities, roles, and career opportunities—is useful for examining the structural aspects of teacher work redesign, it does not adequately capture the nature of the conceptual change that is at the core of revised roles for teachers in restructured schools. In order to complete the picture, I must directly address this aspect of work design, as well as the closely related area of a professional work environment (see Figure 3.1). In trying to understand the conceptual core of restructured teacher work, the classification system developed by McCarthey and Peterson (1989) is especially helpful. According to these analysts, the categories of teacher as colleague, teacher as decision maker, teacher as leader, and teacher as learner capture the essence of the new roles for teachers in restructured schools (see also Barth, 1989). In addition, as I discussed at the outset of this chapter, a number of analysts have emphasized the idea of teacher as generalist in developing their conceptual picture of redesigned teacher work. In shorthand form, I use the metaphor of teacher as leader (see Figure 2.1) to capture the totality of these other concepts. Each of these conceptual dimensions represents a significant shift in conventional ways of thinking about teachers and teaching. In conventional practice, teachers are entrepreneurs of their own classrooms. They orchestrate their own operations almost totally independently of their peers and engage in few leadership or decision-making activities outside their own cubicles. They are viewed as pedagogical specialists whose function it is to deliver educational services to their young charges. Little time and energy are available for or devoted to self-renewal and professional growth (see Goodlad, 1984; Lortie, 1975; Sizer, 1984).

McCarthey and Peterson (1989) sketch a very different portrait of the teaching function in restructured schools (see also Carnegie Forum, 1986; Holmes Group, 1986; Sizer, 1984; Wise, 1989). According to them, teachers are professionals who engage in regular, and important, exchanges with their colleagues—"traditional isolation among teachers in schools begins to break down" (p. 6). Teachers participate in decisions affecting the entire school and frequently perform leadership tasks—in Sykes and Elmore's terms, the managerial role of teachers is institutionalized. They understand that to perform in this fashion they need to be more collegial, to develop more interdependence with peers, and to share their knowledge with others in a variety of settings—that "they must trade work assignments and work in multiple groups" (Clark & Meloy, 1989, p. 292). They realize that by engaging in learning themselves they "are more likely to facilitate in their students the kind of learning that will be needed in the next decade" (McCarthey & Peterson, 1989, p. 11).

Professional Organizational Culture

The redesign of teacher work in restructured schools needs to unfold within a supportive organizational climate—one that reflects "schools as stimulating workplaces and learning environments" (David, 1989a, p. 21) (see Figure 3.1). This larger organizational climate can best be thought of as one that professionalizes teaching (Elmore, 1988a; Wise, 1989). At the macro level—education in general—professional status is enhanced through efforts to align more closely preparation for teaching, remuneration for performance, and other "occupational conditions of teaching" (Elmore, 1989, p. 20) with the norms and practices of the other professions (Smylie & Denny, 1989). At this level, professionalization also entails teachers' securing control over the profession, that is, teachers' establishing and enforcing their own standards for entry and performance (Bolin, 1989; Boyer, 1983; Rallis, 1990; Wise, 1989)[6] and exercising a larger voice over important macro-level educational decisions, e.g., having significant representation on national reform commissions and projects.[7]

At the micro level—the individual district-school classroom system—a professional work environment is one in which teachers are more concerned with the purposes of education than with implementing predetermined goals (Conway & Jacobson, 1990; Petrie, 1990). It is also one in which they "exercise greater control over matters pertaining to curriculum and instruction and to the way in which the school's resources are employed to support teaching and learning," one in which there is "a decrease in control by authority and an increase in control through professional norms of performance, responsibility, and commitment" (Mojkowski & Fleming, 1988, p. 4). Thus, at the school level, "teacher professionalism can be thought of as a new paradigm for school management" (Wise, 1989, p. 303), one that recognizes and supports local control (Carnegie Forum, 1986; Short & Greer, 1989) and facilitates the redesign of teacher work by reconceptualizing the roles and responsibilities of the classroom teacher. As noted above, "the first step toward a more professional culture is the development of collegiality among teachers" (Rallis, 1990, p. 198).

A professional work culture is one that supports the development of organizational structures that help "break down traditional teacher isolation in the classroom" (Bredeson, 1989, p. 11; see also Newmann, Rutter, & Smith, 1989; Rosenholtz, 1985) and encourages "collegial interaction around problems of practice" (Elmore, 1989, p. 23; Giroux, 1988). This type of environment, which characterizes restructured schools, allows the staff to exert considerable "influence over the basic elements of instructional practice (time, materials, student engagement, and so forth)" (Elmore, 1989, p. 20) and over school structures.[8] This, in turn, permits staff to address collectively constraints within the workplace that may affect the successful development of new roles and responsibilities for teachers, e.g., inappropriate organizational schedules (see McCarthey & Peterson, 1989).

In professional organizations, knowledge and competence are highly regarded (Elmore, 1989) and growth opportunities are professionally controlled.[9] Therefore, school cultures that support the redesign of teacher work recognize that "excellence in education will be achieved only as we invest in the education of teachers in the classroom" (Boyer, 1983, p. 179). A professional milieu reinforces teacher efforts at professional growth and the norm of continuous improvement (Little, 1982). Florida's Dade County schools provide good examples of organizations that are restructuring their environments to expand teacher responsibility and develop new roles for staff through enhanced professional growth. Staff in Dade County schools have developed an array of avenues—a professional leave bank, an educational issues forum, an educational compact with a local university, a teacher education center, an academy for the teaching arts, a professionalization of teaching task force, and a minisabbatical program—to help teachers grow professionally and to increase their ability to undertake the new responsibilities and roles that accompany the redesign of teacher work.

SUMMARY

In this chapter, we examined the redesign of work in restructuring schools from the perspective of superintendents, principals, and teachers. I argued that efforts to transform schooling will necessitate a reconceptualization of the roles and responsibilities of teachers and administrators, as well as a rethinking of the relationships that bind them together. Consistent with the perspective put forward throughout this volume, I reported that the bureaucratic model currently defining roles and relationships among staff members in schools is being overhauled. In conjunction with this change, prevailing organizational arrangements such as increasing specialization of roles, management by control, and hierarchy of authority are being replaced as the infrastructure of school organization and management. I showed that restructured schools are places where teachers see themselves as generalists, where empowerment replaces control as the primary coordinating function, and where authority is vested with those who have expertise, as well as with those who have offices. In short, I reported that the tenets of professionalism rather than bureaucratic principles undergird restructuring. I also noted the manner in which these changes play out for professional staff in schools undergoing significant transformation—with administrators moving from the apex of the organizational pyramid to the center of a complex network of interpersonal relationships and teachers becoming leaders of learners. We turn our attention next to issues of decentralization of organizational and governance structures. Two of the strategies in the framework—school-based management and choice—are highlighted. In chapter 5, I analyze issues of curriculum and instruction, devoting major attention to the reform strategy of teaching for understanding.

CHAPTER 4

Organization and Governance Structures

Rebuilding excellence in education means reaffirming the importance of the local school. (Boyer, 1983, p. 229)

The more control a school has over those aspects of its organization that affect its performance—the articulation of goals, the selection and management of teachers, the specification of policies—the more likely it is to exhibit the qualities that have been found to promote effectiveness. (Chubb, 1988, p. 38)

No element of restructuring has received more attention than the issue of devolution of authority to the school site. The key constructs in this discussion are political and administrative decentralization. That is, at the core of transformational efforts to improve education is the belief that the individual school community must become the focus of attention, that the resources and authority to change must reside with those—teachers, parents, administrators—who are closest to the learners. In this chapter, we examine authority and governance structures through an analysis of types of decentralization. The chapter concludes with an examination of the five domains of decentralization—goals, budget, personnel, curriculum, and organizational structures. For purposes of analysis, I divide decentralization efforts into four broad categories: changes between levels of the organization (school-based management), changes among roles at the school level (shared decision making), changes between the school and its regulatory environment (e.g., waivers), and changes between the school and the larger community (partnerships and choice).

TYPES OF DECENTRALIZATION

Between Levels of the Organization:
School-Based Management

> The guiding principle being put forward here is that the school must become largely self directing. (Goodlad, 1984, p. 276)

> If significant changes in the educational system are to occur, restructuring efforts must be focused on and driven by the local level . . . the message is clear and consistent: if restructuring is to be successful, it must be building-based. (Harvey & Crandall, 1988, p. 12)

School-based management (SBM) has been defined in a number of ways. In the definitions presented below, those by Clune and White (1988) and Lindelow (1981) emphasize the transfer of authority to the school site; Malen and her colleagues include the matter of alterations in governance structures as well (see Figure 2.1):

> School-based management (SBM) is a system designed to improve education by increasing the authority of actors at the school site. (Clune & White, 1988, p. 1)

> School-based management is a system of educational administration in which the school is the primary unit of educational decision making. (Lindelow, 1981, p. 141)

> School-based management can be viewed conceptually as a formal alteration of governance structures, as a form of decentralization that identifies the individual school as the primary unit of improvement and relies on the redistribution of decisionmaking authority as the primary means through which improvements might be stimulated and sustained. (Malen et al., 1989, p. 1)

When we unpack these and similar definitions and descriptions of SBM, two elements keep appearing: structural decentralization and devolution of authority. Structural decentralization generally entails the dismantling of larger organizational units into smaller, more responsive ones. This strategy is typically employed in larger, more heavily centralized districts like Milwaukee, New

York, and Chicago.[1] For example, in order to "increase broad-based representation in decision-making at the school level" the Dade County public schools restructured from four administrative offices to six regional offices (Fernandez, 1989, pp. 26–27). In an effort to bring instructional support closer to the individual school, Milwaukee public schools reorganized into six service areas (Snider, 1989, February 8). These structural changes are usually accompanied by a reduction in the number of levels in the hierarchy and in the number of middle-management personnel (Sickler, 1988). As noted in chapter 3, employees who formerly occupied these middle-management roles are sometimes reassigned to support functions in individual schools (Snider, 1989, February 8). In other cases, the money used to fund these positions is freed up to support new initiatives at the site level (Sickler, 1988). In addition, individual schools in structurally decentralized systems may have the freedom to avoid using the remaining hierarchical system. In Dade County, for example, schools involved in SBM have the option of bypassing regional offices and working directly with the various operational units (e.g., staff development) in the organization (Gomez, 1989). As Beare (1989) correctly notes, this structural decentralization is, by and large, "being modelled upon the modern corporation, the flexible conglomerate which keeps central control of the essential and strategic areas but allows entrepreneurial freedom to the operating units" (p. 20), which comprise the corporation.

Devolution of authority is the fundamental concept in SBM (David, 1989b; Lindquist & Muriel, 1989). Under this system of governance, schools, in effect, become deregulated from the district office (Beare, 1989; M. J. Murphy & Hart, 1988). There are "sweeping alterations in the basic authority-and-accountability relationships" (Finn & Clements, 1989, p. i). The basic message is one of expanded local control and influence, of schools being given greater responsibility for their own affairs (Beare, 1989; Watkins & Lusi, 1989). The strategy of improvement is bottom-up change. Benefits expected from devolving authority to the school site, from making the schools masters of their own fates, include: enhanced concern for equity issues (Mojkowski & Fleming, 1988); stronger educational programs and better student performance (Lindquist & Muriel, 1989; Mojkowski & Fleming, 1988); and greater satisfaction among school personnel and constituents (Lindquist & Muriel, 1989).

Among Roles at the School Level: Shared Decision Making

> The possibility of a real reformation rests squarely upon our ability and willingness to reconceptualize the role and authority of teachers. (Soltis, 1988, p. 241)

> [The] primary recommendation is that Americans restore to teachers and to their particular students the largest share of responsibility for the latters' education. (Sizer, 1984, p. 4)

School-based management is primarily an alteration in organizational arrangements in school districts. Authority and influence are passing from higher to lower levels of the organization. As noted above, structural changes often accompany this devolution of authority. To redistribute authority between organizational levels is one thing. However, to reallocate newly acquired influence among actors at the school level is quite another (see Lindelow, 1981).[2] Therefore, I consider shared decision making, or the distribution of devolved authority among members of the school community, as a separate aspect of restructuring.

Strategies to expand teachers' roles in decision making are key components of most restructuring reform reports.[3] Resting upon assumptions (1) about the professional nature of teaching

> By its very nature a profession involves . . . considerable autonomy in decision making (Goodlad, 1984, p. 194),

(2) about the moral dimension of education (see Goodlad, Soder, & Sirotnik, 1990)

> My basic assumption is that teachers should be empowered because teaching is a moral activity. Moral agents, to be responsible for their acts, must be free to act according to their best judgment (Bolin, 1989, p. 82),

and (3) upon the market philosophy of bringing the product as close as possible to the customer

> Every decision about learning and instruction that can be made by a
> local school faculty must be made by that faculty. Teachers know
> what individual students need to succeed better than any decision-
> makers who are far removed from the classroom (Harvey & Cran-
> dall, 1988, p. 31),

there is a growing belief that real educational improvement is dependent upon empowering teachers to lead (see Figure 2.1).[4]

The goal is to move away from a position in which teachers
are treated as hired hands (Sizer, 1984), or property (Beare, 1989),
or assembly line workers (Purpel, 1989), to one in which change
is teacher driven, not authority driven (Soltis, 1988; Wise, 1989).
Restructuring strategies in this area employed to date include: (1)
providing teachers with formal decision-making authority and
other avenues of influence (Conley, 1988, 1989) to help them share
in school governance and gain control over their work environment, especially school-level structures over which they have historically exercised minimal control (Casner-Lotto, 1988; Short &
Greer, 1989); (2) establishing opportunities for professional development (Mojkowski & Fleming, 1988; Sickler, 1988); and (3) creating norms at the district level that support teacher professionalism
(Casner-Lotto, 1988; Sickler, 1988). Although I take up issues re-
lating to models of shared decision making and the potential effects of these efforts in the final section of this book, I note here
that shared decision making often increases the "tendency to
reach *market* solutions to resource allocation in schools" (Carnoy
& MacDonell, 1990, p. 51) and leads to situations in which principals become more accountable to teachers and in which there is a
blurring "of traditional lines of organizational hierarchy and notions of authority" (Bredeson, 1989, p. 11; see also Rallis, 1990).

Between the School and Its Regulatory Environment

> In a phrase, we want to swap red tape for results. (Text of Final
> Summit Statement, 1989, October 4)

> Support for risk taking is signaled by allowing waivers from restric-
> tive rules and regulations. Without relaxing the multitude of con-
> straints on what schools can do (for example, class size, teachers'
> hours, class schedules, and textbook selection), current practices are
> pretty much locked into place. (David, 1989a, p. 24)

Woven throughout discussions of school restructuring is the belief that schools are so deeply enmeshed in a regulatory swamp of rules and prescriptions that, even if schooling is decentralized and teachers are empowered, local attempts at improvement are likely to be choked off. There is considerable agreement that, as currently constituted, degrees of freedom enjoyed by schools are heavily constricted by union contracts and state and federal regulations. Since freedom from external controls is a key piece of transformational reform, both of these organizational–environmental constraints are receiving a good deal of attention in discussions about restructuring the American educational system.

Union contracts. A number of analysts have concluded that the reinvention of schooling will necessitate the rethinking of the traditional labor-management perspective that undergirds relationships between teachers and school boards. Or, as Rallis (1990) succinctly puts it, "in tomorrow's schools, the priorities of labor and management must become more similar" (p. 202). These scholars have noted that the basic concepts contained in restructuring plans often "strike at the heart of the trade union doctrine" (Finn & Clements, 1989, p. 16; see also Casner-Lotto, 1988). They have exposed the inconsistency between requirements for "flexible responses to the characteristics and needs of students in the school" (Mojkowski & Fleming, 1988, p. 6) and the traditional contractual tenets that mandate sameness for all (Finn & Clements, 1989).

Efforts to address the impediments imposed by conventional management-labor working arrangements have taken two forms to date. The first, and more radical, consists of attempts to enhance SBM and shared decision making by replacing the industrial bargaining model with new foundations for relations between teachers and administrators—" to break free of conventional collective bargaining and form a partnership to encourage school improvement" (Bradley, 1990, March 7, p. 10). These systemic efforts fundamentally alter the underlying principles and conceptual frameworks employed in exchanges between labor and management. While it is difficult to describe these incipient efforts fully, I know that the foundations upon which they rest are cooperation and professionalism as opposed to self-interest and bureaucratic control. Labor–management issues are worked out in a problem-solving rather than an adversarial environment (Bradley, 1990, March 7; D. Cohen, 1990). Pittsburgh, Rochester, Hammond, and Dade County are places where a professional model is replacing an industrial view of exchanges between teachers and administrators (see Casner-Lotto, 1988; Sickler, 1988):

> Union leaders in Dade County, Rochester, Cincinnati, and Boston have challenged their members and school officials to confront their districts' problems and to embark on collaborative reform. They have employed new approaches to bargaining and experimented with new forms of agreements. (Moore-Johnson, 1989, pp. 21–22)

The "trust agreements" being employed in a number of California school districts appear to fit this first category of ways of altering traditional management–labor relations (see Kerchner, 1989). So does the "living contract" approach to negotiations being implemented in Hammond, Indiana (Bradley, 1990, March 7).

The second, and more pervasive, method being employed to address limitations imposed by labor contracts on site-level autonomy involves the use of waivers. In this strategy, the basic contract remains in place, but individual schools are free to request exemptions from some of its provisions, e.g., restrictions on class size or length of the teaching day (see David, 1989a; Elmore, 1988a). Many of the school districts that are pioneering restructuring efforts are using waivers from the labor contract to enhance SBM. For example, the teachers and administrators in Hammond, Indiana, now work under a negotiated agreement that allows teachers "on a school-by-school basis . . . [to] set aside elements of their contract in order to implement school improvement plans" (Casner-Lotto, 1988, p. 350).[5]

State and federal regulations.   Freedom from district level controls and restrictions imposed by union contracts will lead to only marginal increases in local options if state and federal government agencies continue to ensnarl schools in ever-expanding webs of regulations and prescriptions—a point made nicely by U.S. Representative Peter Smith after the 1989 educational summit:

> I think that the summit substantially improved the climate for changing national federal policy in regard to schools. The belief

among governors is that you can't get better performance unless you give schools more control over what they do. (J. A. Miller, 1989, October 11, p. 14)

A three-pronged strategy is being used to address the limitations that federal and state regulations impose on school-based decision making. The most far-reaching of these—full deregulation—involves promoting SBM by pulling back the entire regulatory framework. Under this model, schools are provided (or asked to provide) goals and are held accountable for results. In turn, they are given considerable discretion in selecting the processes, strategies, and activities they will use to reach objectives. North Carolina's 1989 School Improvement and Accountability Act is the most comprehensive example of statewide deregulation. Under the provisions of this law, school districts volunteer to participate and those that do "receive money for instructional materials, supplies and equipment, textbooks, testing support, and driver education in a lump sum, to be spent as each wishes" (Bradley, 1989, September 6). In return, they are held accountable for reaching 75 percent of their goals. A more widely accepted version of this model, employed in South Carolina and Maryland, involves deregulating only the top-performing districts. For example, in South Carolina, "schools with a history of superior academic achievement [about 10%] will automatically be released from numerous state regulations governing staffing, class scheduling, and class structure" (Flax, 1989, November 22, p. 1), as well as from a variety of restrictions in the deployment of personnel (Flax, 1989, February 15, November 22). Thus, while North Carolina frees all schools from a variety of regulations, South Carolina and Maryland focus on those that have already proven themselves.

Reducing the number of prescriptions and rules promulgated by government units—enhanced flexibility—is the second avenue being pursued to increase local autonomy. Agencies employing this strategy are examining their regulatory framework to identify where they can cut back on rules—where they can eliminate some of the overregulation in education (see Newman, 1989). The goal is to hasten the pace of innovation by providing additional flexibility to districts. At the state level, a systematic process to clean up the regulatory apparatus is under way in New York. At the federal level, the recent educational summit conducted by Presi-

dent Bush and the nation's governors has touched off a flurry of
activity designed "to examine federal regulations under current
law and to move in the direction of greater flexibility . . . [and to]
provide state and local recipients greater flexibility in the use of
federal funds, in return for firm commitments to improve levels of
education and skill training" (J. A. Miller, 1989, October 4, p. 12;
see also J. A. Miller, 1989, April 19, May 24, October 11, November 22).

Granting schools and districts exemptions to existing regulations—waivers—is the third, most widely used, and newest tool
in the state arsenal of strategies to facilitate local control. Waivers
at this level operate in a fashion parallel to those between management and unions at the district level. That is, under enabling legislation passed in many states in the late 1980s, schools and districts can "request waivers from state law and regulation that they
see as constraining their ability to accomplish their objectives" (Elmore, 1988a, p. 16).

Between the School and the Larger Community:
Parental Empowerment, Expanded Community, Choice

> Consistent across restructuring efforts is the emphasis on increasing
> the active (as opposed to superficial) involvement of parents in the
> education of their children. . . . Additional emphasis has also been
> placed on moving beyond parents to raise the level of involvement
> and commitment of other community members as well. Partner-
> ships—with area businesses and local colleges and universities—are
> playing an increasingly important role in efforts to redesign the
> country's schools. Community support and commitment are impor-
> tant factors to success. (Harvey & Crandall, 1988, p. 14)

In Figure 2.1, parents are portrayed as one of the key groups
of players and choice as one of the main strategies in restructuring
proposals. Changes in governance structures and authority flows,
in turn, are at the center of new relationships between schools and
their constituents. These changes are expressed primarily in three
ways. First, restructured schools *empower parents* and community
members (M. J. Murphy & Hart, 1988). As a consequence, parents
are able to exercise considerably more influence over school
decision-making processes than is currently the norm (Academic
Development Institute, 1989; Snider, 1990, January 31; United

States Department of Education, 1989).[6] This enhanced decision-making responsibility is usually captured in new governance arrangements that formalize transfer of authority to citizens in the school community (see 17,000 File, 1989). For example, each school in Chicago is now governed by an eleven-member committee composed of eight representatives from the community (six parents and two other citizens) and three professionals (two teachers and the principal). These committees have wide-ranging authority over the school program, the distribution of resources, and the hiring of personnel, including the principal.

The partnership metaphor (see Figure 2.1) also includes efforts to *expand the school community*, to unite parents, professional educators, businesses, universities, foundations, and the general populace into a collective force dedicated to the improvement of schooling for all children. There is explicit recognition that "to be successful policies and programs cannot concentrate solely on the child but must simultaneously address the needs of two generations—the parent and the child—for they are interdependent" (Jennings, 1990, February 14, p. 8; see also Council of Chief State School Officers, 1989). Embedded in the idea of expansion are two related concepts: enhanced community involvement in schools—by parents, business people,[7] and members of the school community—and schools serving as community centers, providing a variety of services for adults and children (see Bradley, 1989, November 15; David, 1989a; Schmidt, 1989, November 22).

The notion of parental *choice* is thoroughly intertwined in many discussions about transforming the relationship between schools and their constituents.[8] There is a persistent argument afoot that only by breaking the sheltered monopoly status enjoyed by public schools will significant improvement be possible. Thus, many restructuring proponents clamor for the adoption of a market philosophy in education (Chubb & Moe, 1990), with the accompanying open enrollment patterns and choices for parents and students that this move would entail. The executive branch of the federal government has been relentless in its support of parental choice (Walker, 1989, November 8). For example, President Bush noted in a speech at the outset of his administration that choice is "perhaps the single most promising" of the "good and tested reform ideas" (Bush, 1989, p. 24). Minnesota's "access to excellence" program brought choice via open enrollment to the state reform agenda (Pipho, 1989). Colorado, New Jersey, Arkansas, Iowa, Nebraska, Ohio, Washington, and Idaho have followed Minnesota's lead (Jennings, 1989, May 10; Snider, 1990, April 11; Walker, 1989, December 6; Walsh, 1990). Pioneering districts such as Richmond, California, and New York City's District 4 have paved the way for others with their comprehensive choice plans (Snider, 1989, November 1, December 13). In all these cases, there is a significant transfer of authority to parents. They, not the professional staff, assume responsibility for determining which schools their children will attend.

DOMAINS OF DECENTRALIZATION

The consistent aim which links the changes and proposals for change into a coherent policy shift is to dismantle much of the central administrative structure and hand over to individual schools responsibility for curriculum planning and, ultimately, for financial and personnel management. (Watt, 1989, p. 19)

In concrete terms, devolution of authority to the level of the school community means that many of the decisions that have historically been made by state or district personnel are now made by school staff and parents—and sometimes by students and general citizens. When decentralization strategies such as SBM, teacher empowerment, and choice are employed, actors at the school site gain considerable discretion over five areas of educational operations: three that have received a fair amount of attention—budget, personnel, and curriculum (David, 1989b; Clune & White, 1988), and two that have not—goals and organizational structures (David, 1989a; Short & Greer, 1989). I examine each of these briefly in this section.

Goals. Decentralization of authority provides schools with more control over the direction that the organization will pursue (Carnoy & MacDonell, 1990; David, 1989a). Both the goals and the strategies for reaching them are primarily determined at the site level (Dade County, 1989). Equally important is the fact that the individual school exercises considerable discretion over the values upon which collective action is to be taken (Clark & Meloy, 1989).

This control helps each school develop a unique cultu[...] isomorphic with the needs of the community (Dade Cour[...]

Budget. Control over the budget is at the heart of efforts to decentralize authority. Without the ability to allocate resources as deemed most appropriate by local actors, the other dimensions of SBM lack force. Or, as Lindelow (1981, p. 123) puts it, "control of the curricula and of personnel are largely dependent on the control of the budget." Decentralized budgeting often means the allocation of funds to the school in a lump sum rather than for predetermined categories of expenditures (e.g., a certain amount for books, a certain amount for salaries). This allows the school, rather than the district, to determine how funds will be employed. The larger the ratio of lump sum funds to monies restricted by categories, the greater the amount of decentralization. For example, in Dade County, SBM schools control nearly 90% of their budgets, while other schools in the district determine the allocation of only 10% of their funds (David, 1989a). The freedom to determine whether funds will be spent inside or outside the district represents another dimension of budgetary control. For example, in highly decentralized districts, schools can purchase needed professional development services either from the district's staff development unit or from private contractors (Guthrie, 1986). The ability to roll over unspent money is the final element of site-based control of funds. In conventional accounting practice in school districts, fund balances revert to the central office. When budget authority is decentralized, as in California's Fairfield-Suisun district, schools are able to carry over budget surpluses (Lindelow, 1981).

Personnel. Closely connected to budgetary discretion is control over the defining of roles and the hiring and development of staff. As in the fiscal area, there are various levels of local influence. In the least aggressive model of decentralization, the allocation of teaching positions is determined at the district level. Within this constraint, and subject to state regulations, members of the local school community exercise nearly full control over who will fill these slots. That is, teachers are no longer sent to the school from the district office. Teachers and administrators interview candidates, make the final choice, and pass their selection back to the district. Under more nearly comprehensive models of local control, the allocation of professional positions is not predetermined. While schools are still free to select personnel, they also have the option of using funds budgeted for teachers for other purposes. For example, they can take money allocated in principle for a teacher and use it to purchase books and materials or to hire two or three paraprofessionals (Lindelow, 1981; see David, 1989a, 1989b; Fernandez, 1989; Moore-Johnson, 1989, for examples). In the most advanced cases of decentralization, authority—either full or partial—for the employment of the principal is held by members of the local school community. For example, in Dade County (Fernandez, 1989) and Santa Fe (Carnoy & MacDonell, 1990), teachers are partners in the process established to select new principals. In Chicago, local school councils are empowered to make final decisions about who will be hired to administer the school (Finn & Clements, 1989).[9]

Curriculum.   "Within a school-based management system, the school site has near total authority over curriculum matters. Within broad outlines defined by the board [and the state], the individual schools are free to teach in any manner they see fit" (Lindelow, 1981, p. 122). School-based curriculum (Clune & White, 1988) means that each school staff decides what teaching materials are to be used, as well as the specific pedagogical techniques that are to be emphasized (Clune & White, 1988; Watkins & Lusi, 1988). It also means that the principal and teachers at the school site "determine which staff development activities best meet the needs of their particular school" (Guthrie, 1986, p. 308).

Organizational structures.   Structures within which the educational process unfolds represent a final area of control for teachers, administrators, and parents in decentralized school systems. These groups are free to alter the basic delivery structure in schools, to develop alternatives to the model of the individual teacher working with groups of 25 to 35 students in 50-minute time blocks. At the elementary level, schools are creating educational programs that dramatically change the practices of grouping children by age for classes and by ability for instruction. At the secondary level, a number of decentralized schools are experimenting with alternative programs, core curricula, and outcome-based education (see Murphy & Evertson, 1990, for examples).

SUMMARY

In this chapter, we examined what is perhaps the most thoroughly discussed element of restructuring—the political and administrative decentralization of school organizations. Grounded in lessons from successful corporate enterprises, knowledge of school improvement, and the tenets of professionalism, the following principle rests at the heart of the restructuring schools movement: that the authority to make changes and the control of the resources to do so must reside with those who are closest to the learners. Not surprisingly, we saw that the individual school community has become the focus of attention in experiments to restructure the educational enterprise. In the area of political decentralization, efforts are afoot to provide parents with greater choice in determining where their children attend school and with more influence in shaping the educational experiences they receive while there. Significant changes are also occurring between the school and its larger regulatory environment. Experiments in deregulation such as reducing rules promulgated by state and federal governments and granting waivers to exempt schools from existing regulations are under way throughout the country. Additional degrees of freedom for local schools are also being realized in those districts in which the industrial bargaining model, which has formed the core of management–labor relations, is being replaced with partnership arrangements more consistent with the principles of professionalism that undergird school restructuring. In the area of administrative decentralization, we examined how school-based management and shared decision-making arrangements are beginning to place into the hands of local communities the authority needed to be largely self-directing. I reported that the greater the devolution of authority, the more control parents, teachers, and administrators at the local site exercise over the goals of budget, personnel, curriculum, and organizational arrangements of the school.

CHAPTER 5

The Core Technology

What students are expected to know and be able to do, how knowledge is organized for student learning, the kinds of instructional methodologies employed, how school time is structured, and the relationship of student grouping to learning are all critical variables concerning the nature and organization of curriculum and instruction. For too long these variables have been perceived by many policymakers and educators as constants—unchangeable—that is, traditional schooling has taken on a standardization which has remained long unchallenged. If schooling is to be restructured for improved learning, then it must be challenged. (Council of Chief State School Officers, 1989, p. 18)

Of the various strategies to transform education, restructuring teaching and learning has received the least amount of attention, both in reform reports and in state, district, and school-level efforts to restructure schools: "Few reform reports have touched on the heart of the educational process, what is taught and how it is taught" (National Governors' Association, 1989, p. 1). Teacher empowerment, school-based management, and choice have been the topics of greatest interest (Ericson & Ellett, 1989; Evertson et al., 1990; Hawley, 1988; Mojkowski & Fleming, 1988). In addition, these other three restructuring strategies are increasingly being treated as ends in themselves rather than as means to improved learning for students (Council of Chief State School Officers, 1989). In this chapter, I set out to expand our understanding of restructuring the core technology of schools. I begin by outlining five ways of knowing about revisions in educational processes. Then, I examine in detail each of the five areas in a restructured core technology: student as worker, curriculum, instruction, equity, and delivery structures. For each of these topics, I analyze how current operating procedures are likely to be altered in schools of the future.

Serious efforts to restructure teaching and learning in schools require "bringing the structure of classrooms and schools into conformity with the best available knowledge about teaching and learning" (Elmore, 1989, p. 15). This necessitates a thorough understanding of what constitutes good curriculum and instruction. The knowledge about effective pedagogy that informs our discussion is derived from five related sources: (1) the burgeoning research base on learning, especially new perspectives on cognition; (2) national reform reports and studies from educational groups, especially curricular documents; (3) interviews with teachers and principals that reveal their perceptions about appropriate educational processes in restructured schools; (4) analogs developed from examining other areas of restructured schools (e.g., if in restructured schools, teachers are empowered, work more collegially, and exercise new degrees of freedom, we might expect to find more cooperative student work and additional choices for learners than is currently the norm in most schools); (5) information flowing from states and districts that are pioneering restructuring efforts at the classroom level.[1]

Information gleaned from the five sources listed above reveals that educational practice will look quite different in schools that restructure their core technologies. I envision changes in four separate areas—curriculum, instruction, equity, and delivery structures—designed to enhance the role of student as worker. I examine each of these topics below.

STUDENT AS WORKER

> I began to realize that the teacher was being seen as the prime worker in the educational enterprise and the productivity being talked about was not increased learning, but increased delivery of educational services. If it is increased learning that we want, then the prime worker is not the teacher—it is the student. (Seeley, 1980, p. 7)

At the heart of restructured educational processes is the student. The concept of "student as worker" has profoundly different pedagogical implications than current conceptions of teacher as worker and student as product do (Hawley, 1989; Sizer, 1984; Watkins & Lusi, 1989). All changes in curriculum and instruction in restructured schools are designed to "orient schools and the people who work in them toward serious, sustained engagement in academic learning" (Elmore, 1989, p. 11). We know from a variety of influential studies (Boyer, 1983; Goodlad, 1984; Oakes, 1985; Page 1984; Powell et al., 1985; Sedlak et al., 1986; Sizer, 1984) that such engagement, especially at the high school level, is often conspicuous by its absence—that there exists "a conspiracy of convenience" (Sizer, 1984, p. 154), "a complex, tacit conspiracy to avoid sustained, rigorous, demanding, academic inquiry" (Sedlak et al., 1986, p. 5). Twenty-five percent of all students physically remove themselves from engagement in learning by dropping out of school; another 10–15 percent absent themselves by sporadic attendance; nearly another third avoid work by negotiating treaties, compromises, and bargains with their teachers in which they exchange attendance and compliant behavior for academic expectations. Restructuring of the teaching–learning process by emphasizing the role of the student as worker is designed first and foremost to break this cycle of "pervasive disengagement" (Hampel, 1986, p. 131). The types of changes outlined in each of the four areas discussed below are designed in turn to systematically enhance student engagement.

CURRICULUM

Two fundamental principles must guide the long-term effort to improve school curricula. First, the provision of general, not specialized, education is the role of primary and secondary education. . . . Second, it will always be necessary to make judicious provisions for individual differences in the student population. Most of these should be pedagogical. (Goodlad, 1984, p. 292)

The curricula in restructured schools will be characterized by both greater complexity and greater cohesion. At least seven changes might well be expected: expanded use of a core curriculum, an increase in the interdisciplinary nature of content, emphasis on depth of coverage, use of more original source materials, enhanced focus on higher order thinking skills, expanded methods of student assessment, and additional teacher choice.

Core Curriculum

The belief that there should be a core curriculum for all students is widely held by analysts concerned with restructuring the core technology of schools (Adler, 1982; Boyer, 1983; Carnegie Council, 1989). Critics have exposed the failure of homogeneous grouping and curricular tracking to deliver better education.[2] There is an emerging consensus that what need to be varied are not curricula but rather instructional strategies, or, as Goodlad (1984, p. 289) has stated, "the data on individual differences . . . have more compelling implications for pedagogical than for curricular differentiation." Thus the focus in schools that are restructuring teaching and learning is on helping all students master similar content using whatever pedagogical approaches seem most appropriate to different individuals and groups. A number of pioneering districts (e.g., Cincinnati) have begun the implementation of core curricula (Moore-Johnson, 1988).

Interdisciplinary Focus

The great and urgent need in the curriculum is integration—how students discover patterns and see connections. Yet we continue to organize around the categories of disciplines. (Boyer, in Rothman, May 17, 1989, p. 10)

Many of the reform reports that have noted the "current state of splendid isolation" (Boyer, 1983, p. 114) among the disciplines have been particularly adamant about the need for "a new interdisciplinary vision" (Boyer, 1983, p. 115) "to lessen the splintered view of knowledge" confronting students (Sizer, 1984, p. 133; see also National Commission on Social Studies, 1989). For example, the Carnegie Council (1989) argues that

The key lies in how the student approaches the subject matter. In the traditional curriculum, the student learns subject by subject. This fragmented array does not allow students to connect new and old ideas or to construct their own meaning of the information. In

the core curriculum of the transformed middle grade school, the student confronts themes, which are clusters of subjects, and learns to
inquire, associate, and synthesize across subjects. (p. 43)

Other ways of knowing about restructured educational processes
also direct attention to the importance of interdisciplinary approaches to learning and the need to select "rich, integrative topics" (O'Neil, 1989, p. 3) for instruction. For example, in California,
the new science frameworks reorganize "science instruction by
themes—energy, continuity, patterns of change, and evolution,
for example—that are common to all sciences, rather than by particular topics within each discipline" (Rothman, October 11,
1989b, p. 17). Pioneering schools include Central Middle School in
Murfreesboro, Tennessee (D. L. Cohen, June 21, 1989) and Hope
Essential High School in Providence, Rhode Island (Corcoran,
1989). The restructured curricula in each of these schools emphasize using a team of teachers from different disciplines to work
with a single group of students.

Depth of Coverage

The restructured core technology in schools of the future will
feature a curriculum that will be more vertical and less horizontal.
That is, fewer things will be covered, but they will be treated more
thoroughly (Corcoran, 1989; Harvey & Crandall, 1988; Watkins &
Lusi, 1989). Sizer's (1984) view that "less is more" (p. 89) directs
the ascent from "the swamp called coverage" (p. 131) in a restructured curriculum (see also Goodlad, 1984; Powell et al., 1985,
p. 379). For example, in its recent report on restructuring, the National Association of State Boards of Education suggests that
curricula be altered to underscore the importance of "depth of
knowledge in core subjects rather than acquisition of superficial
knowledge in many broad areas" (D. L. Cohen, October 25, 1989,
p. 8; see also Bradley Commission, 1988; National Commission on
Social Studies, 1989). The Carnegie Council (1989) argues that its
curricular "approach clearly requires that the current emphasis on
coverage of a large quantity of information must yield to an emphasis on depth or quality of the student's understanding" (p. 43).
Hawley (1989) captures the essence of this dramatic shift in curricular focus when he concludes that "instead of trying to cover lots

of different topics, curricula should go into depth on a limited number of issues and emphasize what is called 'generative knowledge,' ideas and theories that help students organize and learn other knowledge" (p. 32).

Original Source Documents

A number of reform groups concerned with restructuring school curricula (e.g., the Bradley Commission, 1988; National Commission on Social Studies, 1989) have begun to call for more use of original source documents and less reliance on textbooks. The advantages of source materials over textbooks have been noted by Boyer (1983):

> Most textbooks present students with a highly simplified view of reality and practically no insight into the methods by which the information has been gathered and facts distilled. Moreover, textbooks seldom communicate to students the richness and excitement of original works. When students are privileged to read the primary sources, they meet authors personally and discover events first hand. We recommend, therefore, that the use of original sources be expanded. (p. 143)

Some pioneering school districts have taken up the challenge:

> At Central Park East, reliance on text books and standardized curriculum has been eliminated, and teachers rarely use standardized curricula or materials. Instead, teachers have developed their own thematic curriculum units and use literature to teach reading and writing, while engaging students in reading paperback or trade books as opposed to basal readers. (McCarthey & Peterson, 1989, p. 18)

> Gowler and the school's staff design and continually refine most of their own instructional materials, and they design according to the students' needs. They do not use any major publisher's curricula in the building. (Lindelow, 1981, p. 15)

Higher Order Thinking Skills

The restructured core technology differs from the traditional curriculum (see Goodlad, 1984) in the prominence given to higher order thinking skills (O'Neil, 1989). In addition, it emphasizes critical thinking skills for all students, not simply for those in higher ability groups. Finally, thinking skills are presented concomitantly with basic skills rather than after more basic skills are mastered. The goal of reformers is the development of a curriculum that helps all students learn how to learn, that "empowers learners now and for the rest of their lives" (Harvey & Crandall, 1988, p. 31). Consequently, there is "less emphasis on memorization and rote drill and more emphasis on problem solving" (Rothman, May 17, 1989, p. 8), "critical reasoning and higher order thinking" (Carnegie Council, 1989, p. 42). The Ford Foundation's middle school mathematics initiative for disadvantaged students is a good example of an effort in this area. The program works with schools that are "committed to transforming their program[s] to focus on higher-level problem solving skills" (Rothman, October 25, 1989, p. 5). Another example is the new set of science frameworks in California that "put the understanding of scientific concepts before the memorization of facts" (Rothman, October 11, 1989b, p. 17). Schools on the cutting edge of restructuring in Dade County, Florida, have also undertaken efforts to emphasize the importance of critical thinking skills for all students (Dade County, 1989).

Broadening Assessment Systems

The types of curricular changes envisioned within the restructured core technology by teachers, administrators, legislators, and reform analysts—a core body of knowledge, integrated curriculum, a focus on problem-solving skills, and so forth—necessitate a broadening of existing assessment systems to monitor student progress. One such change involves the choice of subjects tested. In schools with restructured core technologies, student performance will no longer be defined solely by student scores on tests of reading, mathematics, and language. Thoughtful assessments will be conducted for all areas of the curriculum. A second change concerns the types of skills examined. The current overemphasis on basic skills and factual knowledge will give way to assessment of the higher order skills stressed in the restructured curriculum (Rothman, January 24, 1990, February 14, 1990). In the schools of the future, students will demonstrate their performance not only, or even predominantly, on multiple-choice tests, but also through more authentic activities such as exhibitions, writing exercises, and the compilation of portfolios (Newman, 1989; Rothman, September 13, 1989, February 14, 1990). More attention will also be given to assessing sustained student performance. Finally, new formats for assessment (e.g., teams of students solving problems together outside the classroom) will be more likely to be found in restructured schools than in more traditionally organized schools.

Teacher Choice

Teacher choice in creating learning experiences, with the consequent variety of materials, undergirds much of what I have already presented about restructuring school curricula (Harvey & Crandall, 1988; McCarthey & Peterson, 1989). Teachers assume much more control over textbook selection (Boyer, 1983; McCarthey & Peterson, 1989) and curriculum development (Corcoran, 1989; David, 1989a, 1989b) in restructured schools. Ultimately, "they would teach according to their own beliefs using the instructional material that they had individually chosen for their particular setting. Eventually, they would become the major recognized determiners of the curriculum" (Lindelow, 1981, p. 126).

INSTRUCTION

Most children assume that knowledge just happens to them, that it is handed to them by some parentlike seer as if it were a peanut butter and jelly sandwich. (Sizer, 1984, p. 3)

The focus of schooling must shift from teaching to learning. (Carnegie Forum, 1986, p. 38)

Instructional changes in schools that restructure their educational processes will be as comprehensive and radical as the curricular alterations, discussed above, are. The most fundamental revision will be a shift from teacher-centered to learner-centered pedagogy. The emphasis will be on the student, not on the delivery system. Students will be seen as "producers of knowledge" and teachers "as managers of learning experiences" (Hawley, 1989, p. 32; see also Seeley, 1980). The "jugs and mugs" perspective on teaching will cease to hold sway (Hawley, 1989; Seeley, 1988). A focus on acquiring information will be replaced by a concern for ability to use knowledge. Teachers will no longer be "in the coverage business but in the learning success business" (Spady, 1988, p. 7). Elmore (1988a) captures the essence of this restructured pedagogy when he notes that:

> Prevailing notions of "normal practice" in schools—teaching is telling, knowledge is the accumulation of facts, and learning is recall—will have to be replaced by more powerful ideals that emphasize the role of the teacher as empowering and enabling students to take control of their own learning, and of students as increasingly responsible for their own intellectual and moral development. (p. 1)

In this revised approach teachers will act as facilitators (McCarthey & Peterson, 1989), modelers (Spady, 1988), and coaches (Sizer, 1984) who invest "students with increased power and responsibility for their own learning" (Elmore, 1988a, p. 3). This restructured pedagogical system is perhaps best captured by the label "teaching for understanding" (Elmore, 1988a, p. 11).

The limited teacher-directed model of instruction that has dominated traditional classrooms (see Goodlad, 1984; Powell et al., 1985; Sizer, 1984) gives way to a greater variety of approaches when teaching for understanding is stressed (D. L. Cohen, October 25, 1989; Passow, 1988; Rothman, June 21, 1989). Instruction becomes less generic and more personalized—"coaching, tailoring, and individualizing are all frequently referenced approaches" in pedagogical restructuring efforts (Harvey & Crandall, 1988, p. 13; see also Houston, 1989). Rather than suppressed, the complexity of teaching is recognized and built upon in initiatives to revise the core technology (see Bradley, September 13, 1989a, 1989b).

Cooperative approaches to learning in which students work together in teams are stressed by almost everyone connected with restructuring teaching and learning (David, 1989a). For example, in their effort to restructure educational processes, one pioneering junior high school in Los Angeles has adopted the "team/small group model" of instruction from Germany. In this model "most classroom instruction takes place in table groups made up of from four to six students of varying academic abilities and social backgrounds" (Viadero, November 1, 1989, p. 18).

As with curriculum, teachers are allotted considerable discretion over pedagogy in schools in which the teaching–learning process is reformed (Bolin, 1989; Carnegie Forum, 1986; Wise, 1989). It is also envisioned that the conditions to allow teachers to exercise this control—significantly fewer students, additional time to reflect and plan, more enlightened administrative leadership, additional influence over school-level decision-making—will characterize schools that restructure their approaches to teaching (American Association, 1988; National Commission for Excellence in Teacher Education, 1985; National Governors' Association, 1987; National Science Board, 1983).

Instruction in restructured classrooms is not only more cooperative for students but also more collegial for faculty (National Governors' Association, 1986). Many school systems at the forefront of restructuring efforts (e.g., Rochester) are developing differentiated staffing arrangements similar to those proposed by the Carnegie Forum (1986) and the Holmes Group (1986). Others are developing alternative structures within the school—small houses of teachers and students—to personalize schooling (Viadero, November 1, 1989). In addition, partially in response to the need for planning and delivering integrated curricula, teachers in a number of schools are creating team teaching approaches to instruction (see Corcoran, 1989; Moore-Johnson, 1989). Finally, as a consequence of the professionalization of teaching, instructors are acting less like individual entrepreneurs (see Lortie, 1975; Rosenholtz, 1985) and more like members of a partnership. All of these forces are combining to enhance cooperative pedagogical approaches among the teaching core in restructured schools.

EQUITY

And in the debate about public schools equity must be seen not as a chapter of the past but as the unfinished agenda of the future. To expand access without upgrading schools is simply to perpetuate discrimination in a more subtle form. (Boyer, 1983, p. 6)

No subject is more important to providing quality education for minorities than the restructuring of schools. (Quality Education for Minorities Project, 1990, p. 3)

A third series of changes commonly suggested for the core technology of restructured schools focuses on the issue of equity. At the core of these revisions is a renewed concern for the education of *all* students, especially those who have been ineffectively served in the past—the so-called "at risk" students. This interest has arisen for two major reasons. The first is economic. For the first time in our history we are facing the economic imperative to educate all students to relatively high levels of performance. The surplus of workers is shrinking while levels of competence required in the workplace are increasing. A good education for all seems to be economically desirable (Murphy, 1989b; Seeley, 1988). At the same time, the deeply ingrained belief that the role of schooling is to sort students into two groups—those who will work with their heads and those who will toil with their hands (see Goodlad, 1984, p. 142)—is being challenged. A fundamental shift in the underlying model of learning is occurring in schools engaged in restructuring for equity. There is movement away from a psychologically based model of learning that emphasizes the innate capacity of the student to a sociological framework that underscores the importance of the conditions of learning (see S. K. Miller & Brookover, 1986). With this development, acceptance of the belief that all students can learn has increased and important efforts to restructure schooling (and society) to implement this new view of learning are under way:

> Up to now, the actual operating goal of American society—whatever the ideal of rhetoric, or the commitment of individual schools or teachers—has been to provide educational services for all children, but to expect a "bell curve" distribution of success, with large numbers of children falling in the "mediocre" or "failure" range. Although the change is coming in part because powerful business interests have concluded that the current goal is inadequate for a successful economy, the new goals being articulated are not for narrow vocational training, or minimal literacy for reading job manuals, but "higher order thinking skills" and even "liberal education" for all children. As the Carnegie Foundation Task Force Report puts it, it means "our schools must graduate the vast majority of their students with achievement levels long thought possible only for the privileged few." Although only a few leadership groups have begun to take this new goal seriously, it represents a significant shift in the

goals for our educational system, and a fundamental component of a new vision, since all other components gain motive force from this shift in goals. (Seeley, 1988, p. 34)

Improvement Issues

Coupled with this new economic imperative and fundamental shift in beliefs about student capacity to learn is a renewed interest in developing more effective ways of serving at-risk youth. A number of approaches—including, most prominently, the effective schools movement, Accelerated Schools (Levin, 1987), Success for All (Slavin, 1988, 1990), and the Coalition of Essential Schools (Watkins & Lusi, 1989)—have been developed in the service of this goal. What these and other efforts share, in addition to a belief in the educability of all students, are strategies designed to alter many of the routines currently found in schools that disadvantage at-risk youth. Specifically, restructuring advocates attack the teaching of separate (and hierarchically organized) knowledge and skills to different students (e.g., vocational skills to some, critical thinking skills to others) and the homogeneous grouping of students (tracking) to receive that knowledge (Quality Education for Minorities Project, 1990). Equity proponents are at the forefront of the calls for the development of a core body of knowledge for all students, which I discussed earlier (Carnegie Council, 1989; Committee on Policy for Racial Justice, 1989; Goodlad, 1984; Quality Education for Minorities Project, 1990). Districts pioneering restructuring efforts in this area, such as Jackson, San Diego, and Denver, have abolished remedial classes and now require students traditionally placed in these programs to participate in regular classes (Rothman, October 11, 1989a). In order to ensure that students grouped heterogeneously by ability will be successful, restructured schools are also revising instructional approaches. Cooperative learning strategies appear to be particularly compatible with the equity goals of restructuring.

Compensatory instructional programs that separate at-risk youth from their more advantaged peers have also been subjected to strong criticism by educators restructuring for equity (Committee on Policy for Racial Justice, 1989), and pioneering school districts have begun eliminating "pull-out" programs that create this division (McCarthey & Peterson, 1989). Various reform reports have also called for strengthening the social bonds between school staff and at-risk students (e.g., Boyer, 1983). Schools have set about this task by altering organizational structures to provide these students with additional assistance on a routine basis and to create the context in which personal relationships can develop. Suggestions for renewed emphasis on the cultural and ethnic heritage of at-risk students have also been advanced as a way of developing an organizational milieu that supports efforts to enhance equity (Committee on Policy for Racial Justice, 1989; Schmidt, February 14, 1990).

Expansion Issues

Equity issues are not, however, confined to the schoolhouse. There is an increasing awareness among proponents of restructuring that schooling is but one element of a complex web of social institutions that provide American youth with the services they may need to succeed (Cunningham, 1989; Kirst, 1989; Kirst et al., 1989; Quality Education for Minorities Project, 1990). Three interrelated aspects of this larger concern for equity are found in the literature on educational reform. The first—early start education and health services for at-risk children before the age of five—was a major plank of the 1989 presidential education summit (Miller, October 4, 1989). Interest in this area has resulted in calls for expansion of Head Start-type programs and services (Finn & Clements, 1989) and full funding of the Elementary and Secondary Education Act (Boyer, 1983). The second macro-level equity issue deals with extending both the time and amount of services available to students each day, e.g., an extended day from 7:00 A.M. to 6:00 P.M. in which students could receive special tutoring and recreational activities. The third underscores the need to "bridge the connection between the conditions of education and the total conditions of children" (Kirst et al., 1989, p. 28); it focuses on developing better coordination and "collaboration among schools and other social-service agencies" (Viadero, November 15, 1989, p. 6; see also Finn & Clements, 1989; Jennings, June 21, 1989). All three of these broad efforts signal a renewed interest in promoting equity by stressing efforts to deal with the whole child (D. L. Cohen, October 11, 1989; Wehlage, Rutter, & Turnbaugh, 1987).

DELIVERY STRUCTURES

The organization of schooling appears to proceed as if we had no relevant knowledge regarding the development of children and youth. (Goodlad, 1984, p. 323)

The structure is getting in the way of children's learning. (Sizer, 1984, p. 205)

Efforts to improve the performance of schools without changing the way they are organized . . . will therefore probably meet with no more than modest success. (Chubb, 1988, p. 29)

Foundation for Change

Rather significant alterations in the structures used to deliver educational services constitute the final component of a restructured core technology for schools. Changes are designed to underscore the centrality of human relationships in schools, to replace program isolation with connectedness, and to promote personal engagement in the teaching–learning process. They represent a fundamental reconceptualization of school climate—a shift from an emphasis on its physical factors and toward a focus on its human elements. All of the structural revisions are designed to support, or to provide a context for, the restructuring of the educational processes discussed earlier.

At the heart of these calls for organizational change is an increasing disenchantment with impersonal, time-based, calendar-based learning arrangements. For schools concerned with restructuring educational processes, learning theory and student needs take precedence over the custodial interests of parents, administrative convenience, and market forces (i.e., the need to protect adult jobs in the workplace) in the creation and reshaping of structures to house teaching and learning (Sizer, 1984; Spady, 1988). Calendar-based school organizations give way to structures grounded on three powerful concepts: mastery (or outcome)-based learning, developmentally based learning, and the personalization of learning.

Spady (1988) is an eloquent spokesperson for the first of these perspectives on learning—the need to restructure the core technology of schools around the concept of demonstrated student mastery:

> To appreciate the inconsistency between this sensible concept [organizing schools on the basis of student outcomes] and the way we actually organize and operate schools, we need to look closely at the prevalent practice paradigm: the fundamental character and operating relationships of our system of education. That paradigm is both defined by and organized around the calendar. School decision making, curriculum planning, instructional and administrative operations, institutional arrangements, student certification, and graduation systems, and student opportunity and eligibility conditions— all are defined by and tied directly to the calendar. The calendar and its adjuncts, the clock and the schedule, exert a pervasive influence on both the organization of schools and the thinking of those who work and study in them. Consider these universally accepted terms: school years, semesters, Carnegie units, seat time, credit hours, class periods, grade levels, programs of study, and student eligibility criteria. They all reflect our time-based way of doing business. Even courses, which we commonly refer to as "bodies of knowledge," are actually time blocks that uniformly last nine months, no matter what the content to be mastered or the success of students in mastering it. A "course" ends when time—usually the semester— runs out, not when students demonstrate the learnings the course was intended to convey. In short, we behave as if the entire educational system would collapse if teaching, testing, grading, awarding of credit, and promotion did not follow the calendar-driven two semester schedule. (pp. 4–5)

> In the outcome-based paradigm, it is the outcomes, not the calendar, that determine credit and, in turn, define what constitutes a "course" and the content needed in that course. Here the key issue is reaching the outcomes successfully, not precisely when or how much time it takes to do it. (p. 5).

The second central idea underlying calls for change in delivery structures is a "continuous progress" (Goodlad, 1984, p. 311), or developmentally paced, approach to learning. This strategy "allows pupils to advance from one concept skill level to the next as they are ready regardless of age or grade" (D. L. Cohen, December 6, 1989, p. 13). In order to support developmentally paced learning, proponents such as the National Association for the

Education of Young Children have lobbied for the use of such flexible delivery structures as multi-age grouping.

Personalization, or the humanization of the organizational climate (Harvey & Crandall, 1988), is the third building block on which efforts to reshape school delivery structures rest. The goal in overhauling traditional organizational arrangements, in overcoming the neutrality and peaceful coexistence characterizing human relations in schools (see Powell et al., 1985; Sedlak et al., 1986; Sizer, 1984), is to develop a vibrant community of people—teachers, students, parents, administrators—working collectively toward the same important goals. Personalization of structures facilitates the establishment of positive social bonds between adults and youth (Wehlage et al., 1987) in the absence of which many students are likely to drift through schools (Murphy, Hull, & Walker, 1987; Resnick & Resnick, 1985; Sedlak et al., 1986). This social compact helps to reverse patterns of student alienation (Wehlage et al., 1987; Weis & Hawkins, 1979) and to break the cycle of pervasive student disengagement from serious intellectual pursuits (Powell et al., 1985; Sizer, 1984). The importance of personalization of structures was addressed by the Carnegie Council (1989):

> The enormous middle grade school must be restructured on a more human scale. The student should, upon entering middle grade school, join a small community in which people—students and adults—get to know each other well to create a climate for intellectual development. Students should feel that they are part of a community of shared educational purpose. . . . Every student needs at least one thoughtful adult who has the time and takes the trouble to talk with the student about academic matters, personal problems, and the importance of performing well in middle grade school. (p. 37)

Powell et al. (1985) remind us that

> Personalization has a human and professional dimension. The human side involves knowing students from the point of view of a concerned adult friend, while the professional side adds the element of specialized knowledge about particular strengths and weaknesses in learning. . . . All teachers and indeed all school-based professionals should advise students on a regular basis. Therapeutic skills are

not what most students need from advisers. What they need are adults who know them as unique learners, complex and distinctive. (p. 318)

Sizer (1984) makes the connection between personalization and structure:

Personalization of learning and instruction requires a flexible school structure. A flexible structure implies *a simple structure.* A school day segmented into seven or eight time units, each with its own set of imperatives, is almost impossible to bend. A curriculum represented by six or seven autonomous subjects quickly freezes hard: . . . Furthermore, such a fractionated and specialized set of subjects distorts knowledge for young minds; a simpler, more cogent organization of subject matter is wise. (pp. 216–217)

Micro-Level Strategies

Inspired by these three key ideas, reform advocates have suggested an array of changes in educational delivery systems consistent with the paradigms of "teaching for understanding" and "student as worker." I have already mentioned one of these—a *decreased workload* for teachers. There is a growing understanding that unless current work conditions of teachers are altered, it will be impossible to restructure the core technology of schools successfully (Holmes Group, 1986; National Commission for Excellence in Teacher Education, 1985). Or, as Boyer (1983) has stated, "the push for excellence in education must begin by confronting those conditions that drive good teachers from the classroom in the first place" (p. 155). Some pioneering districts like Cincinnati have begun to lighten the instructional load of teachers by reducing the required number of classes at the secondary level and by providing additional preparation time for elementary school teachers (Moore-Johnson, 1988). Others, like those in the Coalition of Essential Schools, have reduced teaching loads by limiting the total number of pupils with whom teachers can work each day—e.g., 80 students as opposed to the more customary number of between 120 and 180 (Harvey & Crandall, 1988). Still others have reduced class size to more manageable numbers by making more effective use of volunteers and aides and by having support personnel work in regular classroom settings (McCarthey & Peterson, 1989; see also Fernandez, 1989). The flexibility created by reduced loads has been used to promote cooperative planning and instructional activities among teachers, to facilitate more intensive work with smaller groups of pupils, and to allow staff to participate in professional development activities (Bradley, November 1, 1989).

Schools that are engaged in reforming delivery systems have also shown considerable *flexibility* in the ways they organize students for learning. In the best of these, "students are arranged in a variety of ways for various activities and skills throughout the day resulting in alternative grouping patterns for different students and subjects" (McCarthey & Peterson, 1989, p. 18; see also Lipsitz, 1984). At least six different threads are evident in the tapestry of flexible organizational arrangements:

1. flexible use of space,
2. less regimented scheduling patterns,
3. nontraditional grouping patterns within classes,
4. more flexible instructional arrangements,
5. less emphasis on self-contained classrooms,
6. less use of age grouping patterns.

One is more creative use of space (Carnegie Forum, 1986). A second is the use of scheduling patterns that facilitate the development of the social bonds noted above. An example of such a pattern is the use of "home-base guidance" programs in Rochester secondary schools in which "teachers are assigned to small groups of students to establish continuity for the students during their [middle school and high] school years" (Bradley, October 18, 1989, p. 11). A third thread is the use of nontraditional patterns of grouping pupils within classes. In these cases, there is less emphasis on homogeneous grouping by ability and greater reliance on cooperative strategies that more easily mix students of differing abilities, races, and socioeconomic backgrounds (Viadero, November 1, 1989).

Restructuring schools are also beginning to be less reliant on "a welter of 20- to 50-minute segments devoted to separate subjects" (Elmore, 1989, p. 13). They are heeding calls for flexibility in arranging instructional time (Carnegie Council, 1989) and are "discovering that using the pedagogy of student as worker [is] facilitated by having larger blocks of time" (Watkins & Lusi, 1989, p. 5; see also Corcoran, 1989; David, 1989a). For example, some teachers in D. W. Griffith Junior High School in Los Angeles are exchanging classroom time slots and doubling up class periods for more involved activities (Viadero, November 1, 1989). At Hope Essential High School in Providence, the teaching team is employing double periods every other day to present its interdisciplinary curricula.

Flexible scheduling has also begun to crack the self-contained classroom mold in elementary schools. In schools that are restructuring their delivery systems, students are able to move more freely among teachers who are working cooperatively to help a variety of students in the school, not simply those in their own classrooms. Team teaching approaches are also being advocated and implemented by proponents of restructuring in some elementary school settings (Viadero, November 1, 1989).

Lastly, "the tyranny of age-grading" (Sizer, 1984, p. 63; see also Cuban, 1989; Quality Education for Minorities Project, 1990) is being challenged in a number of schools engaged in creating alternative educational delivery processes (Watkins & Lusi, 1989). For example, experiments in multi-age grouping are under way in Jefferson County, Kentucky. In Los Angeles' D. W. Griffith Junior High School, four teachers team to instruct 120 students over the entire three years of their junior high experience (Viadero, November 1, 1989). The Lake George, New York, elementary school has developed a program that "shun[s] the restrictions of individual grade levels. . . . [It] offer[s], instead, flexible groupings that encompass a two- to four-year span, allowing movement between levels for those pupils ready to advance or needing more help in a subject" (D. L. Cohen, December 6, 1989, p. 1). On the state level, Ohio is piloting a program in 12 districts that groups students by skill level rather than by age (State Capitals, October 11, 1989).

Macro-Level Strategies

The restructuring efforts described above are often augmented by more global strategies to alter organizational arrangements for teaching and learning. One of these is the attempt to change the traditional delivery system by *contracting out for teaching services.* "The concept of private practice teaching originated with a group of educators and business people in Minnesota more than a decade ago" (Viadero, September 13, 1989). The practice is consistent with an emerging trend in the business community in which firms are building their operations around a small core of regular employees and then purchasing additional services from private consultants (see Beare, 1989). As Moore-Johnson (1989) has documented, schools in at least one district at the forefront of restructuring efforts have begun to contract out for specialized professional services:

> In response, varying practices are emerging in Dade County. One elementary school council transferred a Spanish teacher who was not meeting the students' needs and hired a Berlitz teacher to replace her. Four schools eliminated the position of assistant principal and spent the salary allotments on after-school programs, supplies, and aides. A junior high school cut eight full-time positions and bought outside hourly instruction in special subjects. (p. 11; see also Fernandez, 1989)

Other macro-level efforts to restructure delivery systems include some of the *expansion strategies* I noted in the discussion of equity. Central to these are revisions to the predominant organizational arrangement in schools—the 180-day school year with instruction delivered from 9 A.M. to 3 P.M. to students between the ages of 5 and 18 living in a specified geographical pocket of a given community. Important challenges to this basic organizational paradigm have been raised by the National Association of State Boards of Education (D. L. Cohen, October 25, 1989), the National Council of Chief State School Officers (Viadero, November 15, 1989), and the Quality Education for Minorities Project (1990) (see also D. L. Cohen, January 10, 1990). Districts pioneering restructuring efforts in this area are involved in: lengthening the school day on both ends; expanding the population served; addressing the needs of the whole student; creating activities that require students to perform useful service in the community; developing more integrated networks with social, welfare, health, and other youth-service organizations; expanding the range of places in which instruction unfolds; and building networks between traditionally isolated individual school organizations. One example of such an effort is the "remarkably successful summer program [in New Orleans] that combines teaching reading to children, strengthening teachers' skills, and providing a visible model of an alternative structure for schools and classrooms" (David, 1989a, p. 14). Others include the use of satellite learning center schools that "are operated by the school district in a facility constructed and paid for by the host corporation and operated on its property" (Fernandez, 1989, p. 15) and the use of Saturday morning classes in many schools in Dade County, Florida (David, 1989a).

> Most of the schools clustering in the top group of our sample on major characteristics were small, compared with the schools clustering near the bottom. It is not impossible to have a good large school; it simply is more difficult. (Goodlad, 1984, p. 309)

The most well-documented efforts at changing the larger organizational structure of schools focus on those schools that have attempted to personalize education by creating smaller and more humane organizations—by *restructuring schools into houses* (Snider, March 1, 1989), by creating schools-within-schools (United States Department of Education, 1989) or alternative programs within schools (Corcoran, 1989). The basic idea here is that each house or program "is to be characterized by its own curriculum, students, faculty and counselors. For most activities, each house is self-sufficient" (Goodlad, 1984, p. 311). The rationale behind this fundamental revision in delivery structure has been nicely laid out by the Carnegie Council for Adolescent Development (1989):

> Schools-within-schools offer young adolescents a stable clustering of teachers and peers. The house creates the conditions for teams of teachers and students to coalesce, for the advisor and students to get to know each other, and for students to begin to form close associations with peers. (p. 38)

This type of organizational change accomplishes three things. First, as noted earlier, it helps reduce isolation and personalize schooling (Quality Education for Minorities Project, 1990). Second, the better schools-within-schools models foster important changes in the basic building block of schools and in teacher orientations. In ideal houses, reorganization is "based on student cohorts rather than content departments" (Snider, March 1, 1989, p. 6), and teachers identify with houses as opposed to departments and/or discipline areas (Carnegie Council, 1989). Third, by bringing about these revisions in groupings and orientations, schools restructured into houses create the context in which important changes in curriculum, instruction, and equity (e.g., team teaching, cooperative learning) are more likely to flourish. Thus, structural revisions have the potential to support, and can often act as catalysts for, significant changes in the teaching–learning process that can in turn enhance active student engagement, thereby creating a learning context for the student as worker.

SUMMARY

Calls from politicians, citizens, and educators for the fundamental restructuring of American public education have dominated the educational reform arena for the past five years. Yet all too often, in their haste to reconfigure the organization and governance of schools, these reformers have paid insufficient attention to the core activity of education—the teaching–learning process. I hold this neglect of educational processes to be a serious problem. I see little evidence that important changes in classrooms will follow automatically from alterations in roles, authority flows, and management structures. In fact, it appears quite likely that these better changes—fundamental as they might be—may wash over classrooms like so many previous improvement efforts. Restructuring must begin with teaching and learning. Other attempts at reform should follow from an understanding of the conditions required to support important new methods of undertaking the basic business of schooling, educating America's youth.

In this chapter, I addressed the issue of restructuring the technical core directly. I began by outlining the five paths we followed in our attempt to understand reformation of teaching and learning. On the basis of that knowledge, I then discussed in some detail the types of changes one might find in schools where restructuring actually penetrated the classroom. I organized the analysis into the five areas of student engagement, curriculum, instruction, equity, and delivery structures. Within each one, I portrayed how educational processes in restructured schools would compare with conditions that characterize technical core operations in traditional schools. When possible, I presented examples where important experiments in reform were under way. In the final chapter, I turn my attention to an appraisal of the restructuring movement as it is currently unfolding.

CHAPTER 6

Concerns and Implementation Issues

The justification given for restructuring often seems to focus on improving the status, autonomy, and income of teachers, and on decentralizing educational decision making generally. It seems likely that many school board members, school administrators, parents, first wave reformers, and other citizens may have trouble understanding why this will improve student learning. (Hawley, 1988, p. 426)

Throughout the earlier chapters of this volume I have raised a series of questions about some of the fundamental planks of the restructuring movement. In this concluding chapter, I discuss some of these concerns more directly. I also examine issues of implementation. That is, I outline those factors that will need to be addressed if the seeds of transformational change are likely to flourish.

CONCERNS AND PROBLEMS

Lack of Attention to Core Technology

Restructuring is a *governance* or *management* reform. (Carnoy & MacDonell, 1990, p. 51)

The relationship between teachers and principals is at the crux of school restructuring. (Rallis, 1990, p. 189)

The development of new roles for teachers [is] on the crest of the wave of restructuring. (Smylie & Denny, 1989, p. 2)

Statements such as these represent prevailing thought in the restructuring movement. It is not surprising, therefore, that, of the strategies of restructuring discussed in chapters 2–5, teaching for understanding has received the least amount of attention, both in reform reports and in state-, district-, and school-level efforts to restructure schools: "Few reform reports have touched on the heart of the educational process, what is taught and how it is taught" (National Governors' Association, 1989, p. 1). Teacher empowerment, school-based management, and choice have been the topics of greatest interest (Ericson & Ellett, 1989; Murphy & Evertson, 1990; Hawley, 1988). Moreover, these three restructuring strategies are increasingly being treated as ends in themselves rather than as means to improved learning for students (Council of Chief State School Officers, 1989; Mojkowski & Fleming, 1988). They are decoupled from the very outcomes they were created to improve. Ericson and Ellett (1989) also point out a key outcome of decoupling reform strategies from the teaching–learning process:

> It is students—their goals and their motivations—that may well prove to be the Achilles heel of the educational reform movement. In other words, we might well improve the quality of the teaching corp[s], legislate higher academic requirements, and reform teacher education to the educational reform movement's content, and yet totally fail in achieving anything close to educational excellence in our schools. The reason will be that there is a nearly total disregard for rational student interaction with the educational system. Students, in rational pursuit of their own ends, are clearly capable of scuttling the educational reform movement. (p. 1)

I find this lack of attention to the teaching–learning process troubling for a variety of reasons. First, I believe that, since teaching and learning form the heart of all schooling operations, then our understanding of educational processes in restructured schools should be at least as well developed as our understanding of school-based management, teacher empowerment, and choice is. Second, our work on restructured schools has led to a very troubling conclusion: the connections between improved educational processes and the other components of change—discretion enjoyed at the school level, authority wielded by teachers, and options available to parents—are tenuous at best (see also Hawley,

1988; Malen et al., 1989). I believe, therefore, that revisions in organizational and governance structures should be more tightly linked to revisions in curriculum and instruction (Bolin, 1989). Reforms should "backward map" (Elmore, 1979–80) from the student. That is, fundamental discussions about how to restructure educational processes for more effective learning should flow from rich conceptions of teaching and learning and should precede the restructuring of other aspects of schooling (Sykes & Elmore, 1989). That is why I featured "teaching for understanding" in this volume.

Lack of Connection Between Restructuring Efforts and Student Outcomes

> The political rhetoric is running far ahead of the evidence. (Association for Supervision and Curriculum Development, cited in Rothman, March 7, 1990, p. 8)

> As the nation embarks on a restructuring of the educational system, it will discover that *sound* new knowledge and *well-tested* products are in short supply. It will also find that many of the proposed "solutions" to current problems have little theoretical or empirical grounding. (Wise, 1989, October 18, p. 36)

What makes the lack of direct attention to teaching and learning in current efforts to transform schools particularly troubling is the fact that the connections between student outcomes and the other components of restructuring have yet to be firmly established. The assumption that empowerment of parents, decentralization of school operations, and the professionalization of teaching will lead to enhanced learning for youngsters has been questioned by a number of students of organizational theory and educational politics, assailed by others, and demonstrated by none (see especially Malen et al., 1989). For example, in his insightful essay on decentralization and choice, David Cohen (May 1989) notes:

> The relations between policy and practice also are taken for granted. Many . . . focus on how changes in the coarse structure of education—finance, politics, and organization—might affect instruction. As in most discussions of educational reform, some direct relationship between coarse structure and practice is assumed. But the re-

lations between policy and organization on the one hand, and instructional practice on the other have been a frustrating problem for US policymakers, educators, and researchers. While connections are regularly assumed and asserted, they are much less often confirmed by research or experience. (p.2)

Despite a good deal of informed opinion about the salutary effects of SBM, teacher empowerment, and choice, the empirical evidence is troublesomely thin. Systematic monitoring of current restructuring efforts such as SBM is rare (Clune & White, 1988). When such monitoring does occur, it tends to be focused on the initial segments of the long path to outcomes, for example, on changes in the attitudes of teachers and parents (Carnoy & MacDonell, 1990; Moore-Johnson, 1989). It is particularly bothersome that an entire movement that is built on the foundation of a shift from processes to outcomes and on an overriding concern for accountability should be devoting so little attention to results and should, like earlier movements, be characterized by an inordinate concern with the search for conforming evidence. Almost unavoidably, conclusions are drawn from early restructuring activities when all the hoopla from the change itself is likely to produce the least reliable findings. In addition, much of the monitoring and assessment to date have been conducted by site level advocates for restructuring—"sources which are potentially biased and admittedly problematic" (Moore-Johnson, 1989, p. 3; see also Lotto, 1983).

Equally disquieting is the fact that rather serious cracks have been found in the theoretical grounding (and informed opinion) for the structural components of restructuring. Perhaps most damaging is the conclusion of Malen et al. (1989) that the theoretical linkages between structural changes (e.g., SBM) and the bridging variables (e.g., teacher attitudes) that connect them to important outcomes (e.g., enhanced student learning)

are neither direct nor dependable, simple nor linear. A host of factors combine to offset the impact of formal structural changes. Some of those factors relate to the characteristics of participants (e.g., their attitudes, orientations, predispositions, skill and will in deploying resources to acquire influence) while others relate more to systemic forces (e.g., deeply engrained norms, the discretion afforded by the formal structural arrangements, the availability and stability of critical resources). Unfortunately little is known about the manner in

which these and other factors combine and interact to shape responses to the formal alteration of governance structures. (p. 29)

Thus, not only is the empirical support for the structural components of restructuring weak, but also the theoretical foundations
may be less firm than commonly assumed. Malen and her colleagues (1989) call for more robust conceptualizations of the theoretical underpinnings of restructuring.

The evidence accumulated so far suggests that there are insufficient data to link the structural components of restructuring—
choice (Elmore, 1988b), SBM (Malen et al., 1989), and teacher
empowerment (Moore-Johnson, 1989)—with student learning
outcomes. In many ways, this should not be surprising. To begin
with, efforts at reorganization—despite the prevailing rhetoric—
often have more to do with politics than with greater efficiency
and enhanced quality. Or, as Kaufman (cited in Chapman & Boyd,
1986, p. 51) succinctly puts it, "the calculus of reorganization is
essentially the calculus of politics itself."[1]

In addition, remember that choice, SBM, and empowerment
represent alterations to the fundamental structure of the educational enterprise. While I readily acknowledge the potential for
structures to shape conditions that in turn influence outcomes
(Murphy et al., 1985; Murphy, Mesa, & Hallinger, 1984), the path
between these macro-level reconfigurations and micro-level processes and activities is long, many-jointed, and loosely linked in a
number of places. Structural changes in and of themselves never
have and never will predict organizational success, i.e., student
learning in this case. It is also instructive to remember that historically, the structural elements that, according to most analysts,
form the core of the restructuring movement have been decoupled
from the teaching–learning process (Meyer & Rowan, 1975). Thus,
in the absence of the type of work discussed in chapter 5 (more
micro-level efforts to address the production function itself and
concerted efforts to link structural changes with classroom processes), analysts should be cautious in raising suggestions that
structural changes—even quite radical ones—will have a dramatic
impact on the outcomes of schooling. As Paul Heckman (cited in
Rothman, March 7, 1990) advised:

> Instead of embracing structural change that may or may not enhance
> student learning, schools should look behind classroom doors and

determine factors that contribute to the kinds of interactions between students and teachers that promote achievement. (p. 8)

I concur. I also agree with scholars like Cohen (May, 1989), Elmore (1988a, 1988b), and Malen and her colleagues (1989) who have concluded "that the relationship between formal structural adjustments and stated objectives cannot be taken for granted. They must be subjected to empirical verification" (p. 30). At the same time, I agree with Elmore's (1988b) contention that to "say that there is no direct causal relationship, however, is not the same as saying that there are no grounds for experimentation" (p. 93). What I have tried to do in this volume is to direct considerably more of the discussion about restructuring toward the connections between teachers and students and to argue that powerful new conceptions of teaching and learning should guide structural efforts at transforming schools.

Potential Disequalizing Effects

Radical devolution of power over schooling must be expected to benefit the rich and handicap the poor. . . . It is hard to see how a serious concern for equity could express itself without a considerable degree of centralisation and uniformity of provision. (Watt, 1989, p. 24)

School restructuring, if it works, will create serious problems of equity among schools. (Elmore, 1988a, p. 28)

While equity effects of choice strategies are receiving some attention, the potential disequalizing consequences of SBM and of empowering personnel at the site level have not been given much consideration. To a certain extent, this lack of attention appears to be the result of the fact that, unlike the first wave of reformers (Green, 1987), transformative reformers have, in fact, highlighted equity issues in their agendas for improvement (Murphy & Evertson, 1990). In addition, these reformers tend to focus on the positive aspects of restructuring for traditionally disenfranchised students and, as noted in chapter 1, clearly acknowledge the economic imperative to reduce the failure rate of the current educational system. Yet some critics maintain that the threads of inequity are an inherent part of the restructuring tapestry. For example, Watt (1989) asserts that self-managing schools "must disadvantage poor children" (p. 23). In analyzing localized curriculum planning, Watt sees "a tendency which seems almost inevitable: to design for schools in affluent areas curricula which will be culturally rich and cognitively demanding, and for schools in poor areas curricula which impose much lower expectations on the students' capacity for intellectual development and hard work . . ." (p. 23). He reports that, since the implementation of SBM in schools in South Australia, there has been an increasing inequality of provision of favorable conditions of learning between rich and poor schools.[2] He concludes that "this increasing inequality of provision is not an accidental and avoidable by-product of sweeping devolution of power, but a central and virtually inevitable outcome" (p. 22). He also notes, quite correctly, that the absence of a centralized curriculum is most likely to harm students who move frequently—typically less advantaged pupils.[3]

In discussing choice and equity, Kerchner and Boyd (1988) point out that "markets are particularly vulnerable to allocating services according to economic class" (p. 101). Elmore (1988b) cautions that what appears to be a neutral policy tool may in fact produce highly segregated schools. He maintains that one consequence may be that "active choosers congregate in one set of schools and inactive choosers end up by default in other schools, creating a stratified system which is responsible to the former and ignores the latter" (p. 95). In a similar vein, Watt (1989) argues persuasively that there are well-entrenched class differences in the ability of parents to exert quality control at the grass-roots level— the very type of control seen by many advocates of choice as providing accountability for school performance (see Chubb & Moe, 1990). Placing control at this level will, he claims, disadvantage less affluent parents and their children. He tackles the issue of equity and choice directly:

> The problem with free market policies, particularly in service areas, is that they almost inevitably advantage the rich and disadvantage the poor. Free market housing or transport policies, for instance, can only mean focusing on providing for those who can pay, and ignoring the needs of those who cannot. The position of the poor in a free market medical system does not bear thinking about; fortunately, we have not yet quite come to that.
>
> Public schools under local control will obviously remain publicly funded, at least largely, but are deregulated and privatised to

the maximum extent possible under public funding. Under these circumstances, increased inequalities in schooling are not an accidental and correctable side-effect of a fundamentally fair set of innovations, but a predictable and virtually unavoidable outcome.

Where there is freedom to choose among a range of different schools, the affluent are inevitably better placed to profit from the freedom and range of choice, by either transporting children to schools in other suburbs or by buying into another area. The poor will in general have no available alternatives. This has, of course, always been so. However, the more diversity in schooling is fostered by devolution of power, the more crucial it becomes which school one has attended. (p. 26)

Funding Concerns

It's true that you can't throw money at problems, but you can't throw words at them either, and that's basically what Mr. Porter is doing. (Robin Zabin, cited in Walker, 1989, November 8, p. 23)

Four financial issues limit our ability to clearly comprehend school restructuring. The first has to do with determining the level of resources required to radically transform the educational establishment. Few reform issues are more bipolar. One group argues that sufficient funds are currently available to support reform. They claim that what is needed is not more money but less bureaucracy and more effort. On the other side of the debate are those who maintain that insufficient resources have been made available to fuel the reform movement (Jordan & McKeown, 1990). Such reformers demand that enhanced effort be conjoined with additional resources. They highlight "the frustration of teachers with the education-reform movement, which is seen as demanding more and more without providing adequate resources" (Bradley, 1990, March 28, p. 11). The most nearly comprehensive analysis to date lends credence to the latter position:

From 1980 to 1988, the country moved rapidly toward funding the first round of education reform that was launched by the 1983 *Nation at Risk* report. The dollars needed to transform teaching into a full profession, the second round of reform launched by the Carnegie Forum and Holmes Group reports, have not been provided. Thus continued education funding hikes are needed in order to finance the full education reform agenda that has been proposed by the country's political, business, and education leaders (at the federal, state, and local levels). (Odden, 1990, p. 45)

Thus it appears likely that efforts to radically reform American education are being undercut by the unwillingness or inability of society to pay for needed changes—or, as Kerchner (1988) has noted, "the cost of the existing educational reform movement is probably well in excess of the capacity of states to finance it" (p. 391).

Compounding, yet perhaps somewhat softening, this conclusion is the fact that very little attention has been devoted to the issue of the costs of educational reform measures. Ginsberg and Wimpelberg (1987) have concluded that "little, if any, attention is paid to the financial or procedural requirements for putting [educational commission] recommendations into practice" (p. 358). Even when expenditures are clearly specified, they usually do not include opportunity costs. In the absence of data on the real costs of educational programs, policymakers are ill informed, and educators and students are ill served. Shepard and Kreitzer (1987) found, for example, that the actual public costs to develop and deliver the Texas Teacher Test—to assess the skills of licensed teachers—were ten times ($35.6 million) greater than the direct costs ($3.0 million) included in the official state reports. In addition, the test resulted in more than $42 million in private costs, including materials and supplies and projected wages for preparation time. In their summary on the issue of costs, they reported:

> A one-time test for practicing teachers was considered to be one of the cheapest of all the likely reforms. Data on the real public costs of TECAT indicate that it was an expense more on the order of a programmatic intervention . . . . (1987, p. 29)

If information on the costs of reform initiatives is limited and somewhat misleading, data to compare the cost-benefits of different reform measures are conspicuous by their absence (Levin, 1987). My concern here is twofold. First, because the amount of money that state legislatures have supplied to date and are projected to provide in the future for reform programs is limited (Odden, 1990), it is important to understand the benefits of investing public funds in differing reform strategies. Without this information, it is difficult for policymakers to make appropriate decisions (Levin, 1984; 1988). Second, the welfare gains (benefits) *and* the welfare losses (costs) that accompany forced collective consumption of government services (e.g., differentiated staffing arrangements, school-based decision making) should be considered (see Oates, 1972). For example, the benefits of differentiated staffing arrangements might possibly be secured through less expensive methods or might be offset by removing highly effective teachers from the classroom for part of the day (Coombs, 1987).[4]

In addition to the less than adequate specification of cost data and the virtual absence of information on the benefits of reform proposals, the "pathetically small" amount of money states are spending to assess the effects of their reform initiatives (Kirst, 1987, p. 163) is severely compromising our ability to learn from restructuring efforts and to make more informed decisions about the shape of the agenda for the future. There is a great need for additional money to fuel data collection activities designed to more effectively inform the policy development process to restructure America's schools (Southern Regional Educational Board, 1990).

Noncritical Adoption of Business Ideology

> The school reform movement at the end of the last century was motivated by the desire to emulate the industrial sector. Many schoolmen at this time regarded the corporate model of school governance as a way out of backroom political control and the way to "organize on a modern and rational plan our great and costly system of public schools" (Callahan, 1962; Tyack, 1974; Tyack 1982). Reformers in the early part of the 20th century wanted to make school administration a science and looked to the literature on business efficiency to adapt to the schools. Administrative progressives envisioned school systems that were run as efficient corporations. (Timar & Kirp, 1988, p. 77)

A number of historical reviewers have eloquently chronicled the significant influence of corporate organizational ideologies and of modern business practices upon schools in the early part of this century (see Beck & Murphy, 1990; Callahan, 1962; Campbell et al., 1987; Tyack, 1974; Tyack & Hansot, 1982). School lead-

ers, in response to tremendous public pressure for better outcomes, and unable to find the solution in their own ranks, looked
outward for guidance. They focused on the efficiency movement
and borrowed its principles of scientific management. What followed in the ensuing four decades were the construction and en-
trenchment of the bureaucratic infrastructure of schooling and the
widespread infusion into schools of the perspectives and values
of the business community. It is these same principles and views
that have come under such stringent attack over the last 15 years
(see chapter 1).

There is little evidence that we have learned from history. As
in the early 1900s, schools are again in a period of intense stress
(Malen et al., 1989)—confronted with highly critical reports of
their operations (see Murphy, 1990a, for a review) and vociferous
demands for improvement. Again, unable to "stem the rising tide
of adverse public opinion alone" (Campbell et al., 1987, p. 33),
educators—especially formal school leaders—and policymakers
have turned their gaze outward for assistance. And again, they
have looked to the new corporate organizational ideology and
modern business practices for their answers (see chapter 1)—mar-
ket-based solution strategies (choice) and decentralized methods
of operation (SBM and empowerment). A careful reading of history suggests that we should be critical consumers of these ideologies of organizing and managing. Two issues in particular are
worth raising in this regard. First, evidence of the effectiveness of
philosophies of management such as decentralized decision making is not much more extensive in the business world than it is in
education—where I have already characterized it as troublesomely thin. Second, a good deal of the evidence that does exist
comes from outlier studies—investigations of unusually effective
organizations.[5] As I have noted elsewhere (Murphy et al., 1985),
the different contexts of effective and less effective organizations
make the routine transfer of findings from one to the other highly
problematic (see also Sykes & Elmore, 1989).

Troubling Contradictions

There is a great deal of tension in much of the activity unfolding in the area of educational reform. As Boyd (1987) has astutely
recorded, there is a schizophrenic quality to much of it. To a cer-

tain extent, this is inevitable. If educational organizations are non-rational systems (M. D. Cohen, March, & Olsen, 1972; Weick, 1976), then to expect change to transpire in an orderly fashion is unrealistic. Or, stated somewhat differently, the rational–structural frame of reference (see Bolman & Deal, 1988) provides a highly skewed and somewhat inaccurate picture of educational reform (Murphy, 1989a). On the other hand, it is becoming clear that in some cases the tensions and contradictions are, at a minimum, delaying real reform, and, in other instances, are actually counterproductive.

One area where this problem is obvious is in the use of policy tools that are inconsistent with the underlying principles of the restructured schools movement. One of the key policies used to effect change—waivers granted by states "to reduce state policy constraints in return for greater school-level commitment to students' results" (Elmore, 1988a, p. 17)—provides a good example. By definition, the waiver strategy legitimizes the status quo. It says, in effect, that the current system is fine and that it is incumbent on the petitioner to show otherwise. As Tucker (cited in Olson, 1990, April 11, p. 19) notes, the waiver system maintains "the current culture because it essentially leaves in place this whole system of rules and regulations that define the real world that people live in." Worse, it (1) continues to provide legitimacy to historically ingrained, and questionable, assumptions about schooling; (2) fails to address the fact that it is often not individual policies but a complex web of rules and regulations that constrain local freedom; (3) reinforces the "picket fence" mentality whereby each office between the state and the classroom elaborates upon formal regulations and contributes to the development of informal norms and accepted ways of doing things that are often more constraining than the original rules; and (4) overlooks the historical use of waivers—by districts and schools incapable of meeting minimum standards (see Olson, 1990, April 11; see also Carnoy & MacDonell, 1990). The waiver system also, again by definition, requires considerable micromanagement of schools by state agencies, establishes a bureaucratic set of procedures and regulations to deal with problems, places power squarely in the hands, not of school personnel, but of state officials, and, not surprisingly, provides little incentive for action.

The waiver system between the state and the district is an

inappropriate policy instrument for transformational reform and sends the wrong messages (see Deal, 1990). To be consistent with the principles of restructuring, the policy selected should convey the belief that it is the status quo that requires justification for continuance. Chubb and Moe's (1990) policy approach to restructuring clearly recognizes the contradictions inherent in employing waivers to reform schooling: since they begin by jettisoning all but the minimal state rules and regulations, there is no need for waivers.

There is also a good deal of tension between the goals and strategies—and residue (organizational sediment and inherited guidance) (D. K. Cohen, May, 1989)—of wave one reformers and the agendas of restructuring advocates (Conway & Jacobson, 1990). While this latter group has expended considerable energy in critiquing earlier reform initiatives, it has devoted significantly less effort to analyzing how these two diverse approaches to reform might be integrated. Change is unlikely to be a winner-take-all struggle between advocates of the two waves of reform: "A happier outcome could result from blending centralization and decentralization" (J. T. Murphy, 1989, p. 809). More thoughtful attempts are needed to show how these two different reform philosophies can be combined to draw upon the best of both while limiting the negative aspects of each—to acknowledge J. T. Murphy's (1989) paradoxical conclusion about well-run decentralized organizations: "successful decentralization depends on strong centralization in certain aspects of the organization" (p. 809) (see also Firestone & Wilson, 1985; McLaughlin, 1987; Porter, 1988).

Finally, there are palpable conflicts among various dimensions of the restructuring movement that have received inadequate attention to date.[6] For example, professionalism empowers school employees; choice (and voice) empowers the school's clients; and SBM empowers site-level administrators and, often, teachers. Each strategy is based upon a fundamentally different belief about who should control public education. To empower one group is not necessarily to develop an organization that is more responsive to the others (Zeichner, 1989). Other tensions are even more troubling: national goals and school-based decision making; teacher choice and core curriculum; curricular depth and national performance (and possibly curriculum) standards. For example, Cooper (1989) points out that some elements of restructuring have the potential to neutralize others:

More seriously, a prescribed curriculum is likely to standardize programs, monopolizing as much as 80 percent of children's time in school and severely restricting the very choices that privatization was designed to offer.

While some beefing up of the curriculum in many schools is probably useful, the government may be undercutting its own efforts to privatize. If all schools suddenly offer the same program, what good are parental choice and local management of schools? (p. 32)

Thompson (1988) speaks eloquently of the tension in preserving diversity in

organization, financing, employment, and curriculum while attempting to assure some standardization of educational outcomes. . . . The reconciliation of measuring outcomes by some standard or partly by standardized measure while encouraging diversity in local educational inputs will require great care at either the legislative or department of public instruction level. (pp. 21–22)

And Rallis (1990) reminds us that

any discussion of teacher empowerment carries with it bedrock tensions between autonomy and control, responsibility and accountability, collaboration and isolation, group goals and individual satisfaction. (p. 194)

Advocates of radical reform have yet to discuss how these, and other, seemingly contradictory elements of restructuring can all unfold simultaneously.

IMPLEMENTATION ISSUES

In many respects, restructuring can be approached in a fashion similar to implementing multiple, intertwined school improvement efforts, with the understanding that they are incredibly more massive and complex. (Harvey & Crandall, 1988, p. 15)

Any fundamental change in school organization will reverberate through these institutionalized roles and interests, altering their positions relative to one another. Whether school restructuring is politically and organizationally feasible, then, will depend on how

clever the advocates of reform are in reckoning with those affected
by restructuring. (Elmore, 1988a, p. 8)

An objective reviewer of previous attempts at educational reform—especially of what Elmore (1987) calls large, glacial changes
such as the restructuring movement—would be unlikely to wager
that the current cycle of reform will lead to major improvements.
Scholars from a variety of disciplines—history, economics, political science, organizational sociology—have developed insightful
explanations to show why and how cycles of reform wash over
the educational enterprise, leaving it largely unaltered (see D. K.
Cohen, 1989, 1990; Cuban, 1990; Elmore, 1987; Meyer & Rowan,
1975; Weick, 1976). Analysts have employed these insights to construct a fairly persuasive case that the current reform movement
will fare no better than its predecessors. However, we enter this
new era of reform with considerably less organizational, political,
and technical naïveté than we had in the past. We have learned a
good deal about both the macro-level organizational and political
factors and the micro-level implementation issues that will require
attention if improvement strategies are likely to take root. In the
remainder of this chapter, I briefly discuss some of the conditions
that will facilitate restructuring initiatives. Whenever possible, I
ground the analysis of the more generic implementation strategies
in the context of restructuring efforts currently afoot throughout
the country.

Readiness—Trust, Direction, and Risk

Shared vision held and nurtured by a progressive school board, superintendent, and teachers' union is essential for the implementation and flourishment of restructuring initiatives. (Fernandez, 1989,
p. 31)

You have to leave room for failure. We're pioneers. (Unidentified
teacher, cited in Moore-Johnson, 1988, p. 750)

This first set of enabling conditions is designed to foster the
development of an organizational culture that will support educational transformation. As Bredeson (1989) rightly reminds us,
readiness is an important antecedent to restructuring. Not everyone will be comfortable with the components of restructuring.

Some in fact will be quite skeptical of what they are likely to perceive as another round of lofty pronouncements, flurries of activity, and marginal improvements. The likelihood of personal loss, especially for those who currently control school systems (Bolin, 1989), will be quickly noted by others. And the potential of restructuring measures to aggravate existing tensions in the system will not be lost on many. It is therefore not surprising that a number of students of restructuring have concluded that trust is a bedrock condition for change (Bredeson, 1989; Casner-Lotto, 1988; Harrison et al., 1989; Schlechty, 1990). One major guideline for nurturing this sense of trust has been proposed by Houston (1989): attend first "to the relational as opposed to the technical aspects" (p. 2) of change. Other strategies extracted from current restructuring efforts include: helping people clearly see the advantages of change (Chapman & Boyd, 1986); recognizing and accepting resistance (Mojkowski & Fleming, 1988); allaying concerns and fears about the unknown (Chapman & Boyd, 1986); developing strong working relationships among groups (Elmore, 1988a); and "affirming each school's or department's status as part of a larger organization" (Harrison et al., 1989, p. 57).

One area where this development of trust seems crucial is in labor–management relations (Fernandez, 1989). Since some of what is contained in the restructuring movement "stick[s] at the heart of trade union doctrine" (Finn & Clements, 1989, p. 15) and "may compel violations of long standing egalitarian norms among teachers" (Conley, 1989, p. 15), it is important that teacher unions feel that they are integrally involved in the entire transformational change effort.[7] As Rallis (1990) notes:

> Since establishing a professional culture will require great commitment on the part of teachers, unions must be involved. Just as the negotiating table has produced contracts that limit the time and responsibility the organization is able to ask of its teachers, it also can be the most effective means to establish new work norms. Through the power of collective bargaining, teachers can achieve more flexible schedules and more flexible accountability systems. The union can build acceptance and support for changes aimed at the enhancement of the profession. Recent research by the Rand Corporation reveals that plans for school change do not become real classroom changes without the participation of a powerful, well-led teachers' union. (p. 191)

Readiness also includes a sense of direction, or purpose, that is widely communicated and internalized by all stakeholders in the change process (Harrison et al., 1989; Schlechty, 1990). It appears especially necessary to create what one might call "a sense of the possibilities," i.e., a belief that something different is possible along with some conception about what those potentialities are (see also Giroux, 1988). The idea of what a school is is so well grounded in the minds of educators and parents that, when provided meaningful opportunities for change, they are often at a loss about what to do (Elmore, 1988a). Teachers and administrators carry a lot of emotional baggage that predisposes them to act in certain ways (Bolin, 1989). Likewise, a good deal of organizational sediment reinforces the status quo, making it difficult to see different ways of organizing and acting (D. K. Cohen, 1989). Also, schools have operated within such a confining web of externally imposed rules and regulations for so long that, even when they are removed, it is hard to imagine how things might be different (Olson, 1990, April 11). Finally, deeply ingrained ways of acting are tightly linked to sacred and traditional values in the education professions (Corbett et al., 1987; Lortie, 1975). The fundamentally conservative nature of this value structure (Lortie, 1975) often limits the development of radical, transformational change proposals. For all of these reasons, a sense of direction must be forged on the anvil of dreams and possibilities of what schooling might become. Systematic efforts—through readings, discussions, and visits to other schools—to expand people's view of what can be done will facilitate the development of a sense of direction for restructuring schools.

The development of a sense of the possibilities is the first step in establishing direction for restructuring efforts. The creation of what Mojkowski and Fleming (1988) call the "grand design" (p. 13) is the second. In effect, the grand design is a long-term plan of operations that captures possibilities in ways that allow people to direct their energies and assess their progress. Grand designs in restructuring efforts work best when they (1) focus on teaching and learning (Elmore, 1988a); (2) clearly delineate the new roles and responsibilities everyone must fulfill in support of the plan (Lindelow, 1981; Lindquist & Muriel, 1989); and (3) address the entire system, i.e., when they require "adaptation and integration by the entire organization" (Moore-Johnson, 1989, p. 23) and when they reach the routine daily activities of the school (Elmore, 1988a).

Finally, readiness entails a commitment to take risks (David, 1989a; Fernandez, 1989) and the right to fail (Moore-Johnson, 1988), conditions not normally a part of the culture of schools (Giroux, 1988). Willingness to take risks in turn is composed of at least three ingredients—the sense of the possibilities noted above, incentives to change, and strong organizational support.

Time

> In short, the new system generated a lot more work. (Lindelow, 1981, p. 103)

> Empowerment via the express route is unlikely to occur in schools. (Bredeson, 1989, p. 23)

Analysts and teachers themselves regularly emphasize the importance of time in restructuring efforts (Radnofsky, Evertson, & Murphy, 1990). Four aspects of this implementation issue receive a good deal of scrutiny. To begin with, reformers argue, time is needed to get restructuring operations under way. Extracting lessons from districts pioneering change efforts, they maintain that transformational reform measures should be phased in slowly (Lindelow, 1981). They report that these districts often begin with pilot projects and volunteer schools before extending restructuring efforts more generally (Dade County, 1989; Lindelow, 1981). There is also the issue of an appropriate amount of time required for results, the need to develop a time frame that is sufficient to ensure that complex changes can unfold and begin to produce desired outcomes. In Harvey and Crandall's (1988) words, "a long-range plan and vision [should] exist as guiding beacons . . . everyone involved must recognize that it is a long-term commitment" (p. 19). Districts that have been successful in empowering professionals and in decentralizing operations have often taken 5 to 10 years to do so (David, 1989a; Lindelow, 1981).

In addition to these two organizational issues of time—start-up time and time to produce results—there are two others that are more individualistic. All the evidence to date confirms the fact that restructuring schools requires additional time and effort from teachers, administrators, and students (Chapman & Boyd, 1986; Clune & White, 1988; Lindelow, 1981). Indeed, commonly over-looked is the fact that restructuring the technical core has a dra-matic impact on student work. It requires students to shift from a passive role to a much more active one (see Sizer, 1984). This, as Corcoran (1989) discovered in one restructuring high school, is a very difficult change for students to make. Everyone has new roles and responsibilities, and the decision-making structure is more labor intensive and complex (Gomez, 1989; Moore-Johnson, 1988). Thus, as Bredeson (1989) has succinctly reported, "time is a key resource for empowerment" (p. 21). If restructuring is to work, schools will need to recognize that "voluntary reprofession-alization has its limits" (Carnoy & MacDonell, 1990, p. 57), that reform cannot simply be added to the already heavy load carried by school personnel, especially teachers:

> We must also be wary of the seductive nature of teacher empower-ment rhetoric. Many reformers are now asking how teachers can be included in decision making and become more responsible for the school's progress. The call for increased professionalism is a noble goal, but let us not replace our unrealistic desire for super leaders with an equally unrealistic desire for a host of super teachers who also serve as super leaders in their spare time. (Rallis, 1990, p. 185)

Developing realistic expectations about what can be accomplished (Gomez, 1989), jettisoning some old responsibilities as new ones are added, and establishing structures to help teachers assume new roles (e.g., released time for planning, summer contracts, ad-ditional compensation) are ways that extra time can be provided (David, 1989a). Finally, because the "structural isolation of teach-ers' work" (Elmore, 1988a, p. 3; see also Lortie, 1975) is one of the major barriers to empowering school-level personnel and decen-tralizing operations, it is important that time be made available for groups to work together (Bolin, 1989; Giroux, 1988)—especially for "sustained collaboration among teachers over pedagogical and curricular issues" (Houston 1989, p. 6). Such flexibility may re-quire structural changes in the school schedule (see Murphy & Evertson, 1990).

Professional Development

> Human resource development becomes the linchpin upon which all improvement efforts are based. (Schlechty, 1990, p. 139)

> When districts delegate authority to schools, . . . [an important first element] is access to new knowledge and skills. (David, 1989b, p. 52)

Undertaking new roles, working in schools that are organized and managed in radically different ways, and, all the while, actively reframing the teaching craft itself represent immense new challenges to educators and community members—ones for which most are unprepared (David, 1989a). Mojkowski and Fleming (1988) report that the training needed to meet these challenges is often either totally absent or woefully inadequate. It is not surprising, therefore, that nearly every analyst identifies professional development as a key variable in the formula for successful implementation of restructuring initiatives (Casner-Lotto, 1988; David, 1989a; Finn & Clements, 1989).

Three types of training appear to be needed to assist educational stakeholders to work in restructured schools. The first centers on substantive issues—undertaking and being able to successfully perform new roles and responsibilities, e.g., developing performance-based assessments for students, acting as a mentor for a beginning teacher. The second deals with the process skills needed to exercise these new functions, e.g., strategies for conflict resolution, group process skills. The third focuses on newly needed technical skills, e.g., the legal procedures that a school site council would need to employ when hiring a new principal (Chapman & Boyd, 1986; Gomez, 1989; Mojkowski & Fleming, 1988).

Administrative Support

> If superintendents fail to take the lead, however, the empowerment of teachers will not occur. (Frymier, 1987, p. 14)

> It would appear that not only is strong advocacy by the superintendent needed, but also a similar level of commitment by the building principal. (Lindquist & Muriel, 1989, p. 412)

If attempts to transform schooling throughout the nation are to be successful, we will need a good deal of patience, wisdom, and trust; more than a little luck; and considerable support and direction from all educational stakeholders, especially formal school leaders. Students of restructuring are reaffirming a lesson learned in earlier studies of school improvement: the superintendent is the "lynchpin of sustaining reform movement" (Finn & Clements, 1989, p. 6). Superintendents, even in decentralized systems, act as gatekeepers for change at the district and school levels. Without their endorsement and support, their willingness to commit valuable tangible and intangible organizational resources, the seeds of restructuring are likely to fall on barren ground. On the other hand, in districts where transformational change is occurring, there is invariably a superintendent who endorses the concept (Carnoy & MacDonell, 1990; Casner-Lotto, 1988; Lindquist & Muriel, 1989).

It is also clear that support from other administrators is crucial in implementing the planks of restructuring. A number of analysts, for example, have noted the capacity of principals to significantly hamper district efforts to decentralize the governance and management of schools (Carnoy & MacDonell, 1990). Others have described principals' ability to squelch restructuring initiatives bubbling up from the teaching core (Houston, 1989). And almost all reviewers find supportive principals in the vanguard of successful school-level restructuring efforts (Bredeson, 1989; Houston, 1989; Moore-Johnson, 1989). Finally, there is some evidence that support of the local school board is needed if transformational changes are to flourish in school districts (Fernandez, 1989; Lindelow, 1981).

Financial and Technical Assistance

> Time is money in teacher empowerment. Time to plan, to interact, to carry out plans is often translated into budget allocations with assigned costs. (Bredeson, 1989, p. 23)

Substantial sums of money will be needed to make the transition from the current educational system to the schools of the twenty-first century envisioned by educational reformers (Carnoy & MacDonell, 1990; Sickler, 1988). It will also cost more money to operate schools once they are restructured (Bredeson, 1989; David, 1989a). The provision (Carnoy & MacDonell, 1990) or nonprovision (Chapman & Boyd, 1986) of these needed resources can have dramatic effects on the success of restructuring efforts. Other forms of assistance include: the development of procedures for the routine analysis and evaluation of change efforts coupled with ongoing feedback mechanisms (Short & Greer, 1989), especially methods of helping teachers use evidence of their "own teaching as the raw material for analysis and deliberation about teaching" (Houston, 1989, p. 7); continuous staff development activities (Harvey & Crandall, 1988); well-planned visits to other schools that have implemented elements of restructuring (Harvey & Crandall, 1988); connecting schools with corporate and community groups; providing incentives for teachers "to do the kind of imaginative and disciplined work upon which new school structures are to stand" (Houston, 1989, p. 20); and "fostering community and political interest" (Harvey & Crandall, 1988, p. 21).

SUMMARY

In this final chapter, I have discussed some of the issues that will need to be addressed as we continue efforts to change American education in fundamental ways. These issues are of two types: problems and concerns embedded in the current tapestry of reform and implementation matters. In addressing the concerns, I underscored a recurring theme of this volume—an overemphasis to date on the structural dimensions of restructuring. I noted that the theoretical underpinnings for the connections between these structural alterations and student outcomes—and the mediating or bridging variables between the two—are considerably less firm than reform advocates often suggest. I also reported that the empirical linkages between these sets of variables are elusive. I argued that it is time to redirect the restructuring spotlight on the classroom and the processes and activities that unfold there. I suggested that the restructuring of the organization and governance dimensions of schooling should backward map from the conceptions of teaching and learning presented in chapter 5 of this volume.

In discussing other concerns and in examining implementation issues, I uncovered reasons to be guarded with our claims about the likelihood of widespread fundamental reform of the American educational system. Schooling today looks a good deal as it has in the past. Given the current organizational infrastructure and political culture of schools, education has a tremendous capacity (and need) to deflect improvement efforts and to respond to change in a ritualistic fashion. Even when goodwill and commitment are widely distributed throughout the system, change is not a foregone conclusion. When new ideas do penetrate the system, they are more likely to be massaged to fit existing conditions than vice versa. There is also a fair amount of evidence that schools have a tendency to drift—or to snap in some cases—back to prechange states of existence. I pointed out at the same time, however, that while our understanding of change in schools is still in its infancy, we enter the era of restructuring much better armed to deal with these organizational dynamics than we were in the past. We also have a much richer understanding of the political realities of education and a willingness to discuss change within that context, however messy the implications may be for change efforts. Given both these caveats and those hopeful signposts, I outlined strategies that schools and educational stakeholders will find useful as they implement the elements and components of restructuring discussed in this volume.

NOTES

Introduction

1. See Ginsberg & Wimpelberg (1987) and Plank (1987) for an analysis of the "commissioned" approach to developing reform reports.

2. Consistent with other reviewers (e.g., Green, 1987; Plank & Ginsberg, 1990), I divide the educational reform movement of the 1980s into two phases or waves. This division is for purposes of analysis only. In actuality, not all reform initiatives cluster neatly into two distinct waves (see Firestone, Fuhrman, & Kirst, 1990, for a discussion).

Chapter 1

1. A case can also be made for greater centralization of services (see Maxwell & Aronson, 1977, and Oates, 1972).

2. The connections between devolution of authority in schools and greater organizational responsiveness and effectiveness have yet to be drawn. In fact, the most thoughtful studies and reviews done to date (e.g., Malen & Ogawa, 1988; Malen et al., 1989) raise serious questions about whether these outcomes are even likely.

3. At least one analyst has cautioned that choice experiments may "impose the risks of mindless and destructive competitiveness without the benefits of greater attention to quality" (Elmore, 1988b, p. 95).

4. Precursors to this current group include Friedman (1955) and Coons & Sugarman (1978).

5. A number of analysts raise serious questions about constructing educational renewal on a platform of economic competitiveness (see, for example, Giroux, 1988; and B. Mitchell, 1990).

6. This same criticism has been leveled at the most widely employed strategies found in wave two reforms (Hawley, 1988; Evertson et al., 1990; Murphy & Evertson, 1990).

7. Critical analyses of bureaucracy in education are not new (see Campbell, Fleming, Newell, & Bennion, 1987, pp. 72–80, for a review of critiques from the 1960s and 1970s). What appears to be different now is that the critics are playing on center court and that a critical mass of dis-

content is near at hand. For analyses of the dysfunctions of noneducational bureaucracies, see Downs, 1967; Elmore, 1979–80; and Morgan, 1986, pp. 35–37.

8. For informative discussions of the school as the center for change, see Murphy, Hallinger, & Mesa (1985) and Sirotnik (1989).

9. There is some question, however, about how widespread this revolutionary change is in the corporate world (see Collins, Ross, & Ross, 1989).

Chapter 2

1. I acknowledge my debt to Richard Elmore's (1989) insightful analysis on "models of restructuring," which guided my thinking on this topic.

2. The changes outlined in this section on the significance of restructuring are not new, and the older views they are challenging have also been questioned in the past. The difference in many of the areas is, however, that

> the conversation is broader than in the past, conducted at the very center of education, and supported by other social forces. The forces may result from advances in technology and cognitive psychology . . . or from larger shifts in economic and social spheres; in any case, these are ideas whose time has come. (Fisher, 1990, p. 84)

Note the influence of so many important reconfigurations unfolding at the same time. Educational restructuring efforts gain significance and power from the context in which they unfold. In short, "the push for restructuring American public schools reflects a global trend to rethink how humans organize themselves" (Rallis, 1990, p. 185). Although I confine my analysis of restructuring primarily to events in the United States, it is clear that it is an international phenomenon as well (see Beare, 1989; Beare & Boyd, in press; Chapman & Boyd, 1986; Cooper, 1989; and Watt, 1989).

3. See Callahan (1962); Campbell et al. (1987); Cuban (1976); Tyack (1974); and Tyack & Hansot (1982) for reviews.

4. This change in thinking can be traced back to early reformers from the effective schools movement, e.g., Brookover and Edmonds. It continues to be one of the fundamental principles of effective schools advocates. More recently developed programs such as Levin's (1987) Accelerated Schools and Slavin's (1988, 1990) Success for All also reject traditional views of how ability is distributed.

5. See Beck (1991) for a discussion of this phenomenon in educational leadership.

precollegiate education. For example, since 1988 the following corporations have made significant financial commitments to elementary and secondary schooling: Coca-Cola Foundation ($50 million); IBM ($25 million); General Electric ($35 million); Citibank ($20 million); RJR Nabisco Foundation ($30 million). Many of these funds are targeted directly toward restructuring efforts, e.g., schools that implement SBM (Flax, 1990). Second, businesses are providing personnel to work intensively with individual schools and school districts (see, for example, Carnoy & MacDonell, 1990). "Adopt-a-school" programs are good examples of this type of activity.

8. It is not my intention here to explore the issues of choice in detail. Readers who wish to do so are directed to Boyd and Kerchner (1988), Boyd and Walberg (1990), and Chubb and Moe (1990).

9. In the first exercise of this authority, 18 percent of Chicago's elected local school councils voted not to retain their current principals (Snider, 1990, March 14).

Chapter 5

1. See Evertson et al. (1990) and Murphy, Evertson, & Radnofsky (in press) for more discussions of these ways of knowing.

2. See Good & Marshall (1984), Murphy & Hallinger (1989), and Oakes (1985) for reviews.

Chapter 6

1. I recognize the facts that not all restructuring changes need to be measured in terms of their effects on student outcomes and that the redistribution of power in educational institutions may be a legitimate outcome in and of itself. For example, David Clark (personal communication) has argued that creating a professional work environment for teachers is a legitimate end in itself. Elmore (1988b) in turn reminds us "that consumer and producer choice may be values worth recognizing in their own right, regardless of their instrumental relationship to student performance" (pp. 93–94). At the same time, however, a reform movement designed to eradicate the student performance problems plaguing education in the 1970s and 1980s needs to be evaluated on its ability to make progress in this area.

2. See Murphy & Hallinger (1989) for a review of research on favorable conditions of learning.

3. Standard curriculum is seen as so critical for minority children that a 1989 research panel called for a national curriculum to help ease the problems faced by migrant students (Schmidt, 1989, November 29).

4. There is some evidence (Chapman & Boyd, 1986) that additional

responsibilities and roles for teachers in restructured schools may carry a heavy opportunity cost—a diminution of teacher effort toward their central task of teaching and learning.

5. Two points of irony are reported here. First, while critics everywhere encourage schools to apply findings from effective corporations, they usually overlook the fact that effectiveness studies—at least since 1970—originated in education. Second, while effectiveness studies in education are often dismissed as nonscientific in the educational academic community, effectiveness studies from business are often held in high regard.

6. Part of the reason that these conflicts have received such little scrutiny is the lack of well-accepted definitions both of restructuring (Harvey & Crandall, 1988) and of the strategies that comprise this construct (e.g., empowerment, SBM) (Bolin, 1989; Mojkowski & Fleming, 1988). As Elmore (1988a) reminds us, once restructuring is better defined, these contradictions are much more likely to surface.

7. For an analysis of alternative approaches to labor–management relations for school teachers and administrators, see Mitchell (1989).

References

Academic Development Institute. (1989). *Building the value-based school community.* Chicago: Author.

Adler, M. J. (1982). *The Paideia proposal.* New York: Macmillan.

American Association of Colleges for Teacher Education. (1988). *School leadership preparation: A preface for action.* Washington, DC: Author.

Angus, L. (1988, April). *School leadership and educational reform.* Paper presented at the annual meeting of the American Educational Research Association, New Orleans.

Association for Supervision and Curriculum Development. (1986, September). *School reform policy: A call for reason.* Alexandria, VA: Author.

Barth, R. S. (1989). The principal and the profession of teaching. In T. J. Sergiovanni & J. H. Moore (Eds.), *Schooling for tomorrow: Directing reform to issues that count.* Boston: Allyn and Bacon.

Beare, H. (1989, September 25). *Educational administration in the 1990s.* Paper presented at the national conference of the Australian Council for Educational Administration, University of New England, Armidale, New South Wales, Australia.

Beare, H., & Boyd, W. L. (Eds.). *Restructuring schools: An international perspective on the movement to transform the control and performance of schools.* Berkeley: McCutchan.

Beck, L. G. (1991, April 11), *Reclaiming educational administration as a caring profession.* Paper presented at the annual meeting of the American Educational Association, Chicago, IL.

Beck, L. G., & Murphy, J. (1990). *Understanding the principalship: A metaphorical analysis from 1920 to 1990.* Nashville, TN: National Center for Educational Leadership, Peabody College, Vanderbilt University.

Bolin, F. S. (1989, Fall). Empowering leadership. *Teachers College Record, 91*(1), 81–96.

Bolman, L. G., & Deal, T. E. (1988). *Modern approaches to understanding and managing organizations.* San Francisco: Jossey-Bass.

Boyd, W. L. (1987, Summer). Public education's last hurrah? Schizophrenia, amnesia, and ignorance in school politics. *Educational Evaluation and Policy Analysis, 9*(2), 85–100.

Boyd, W. L. (1990). Balancing control and autonomy in school reform: The politics of "Perestroika." In J. Murphy (Ed.), *The reform of American public education in the 1980s: Perspectives and cases.* Berkeley: McCutchan.

Boyd, W. L., & Hartman, W. T. (1988). The politics of educational productivity. In O. Monk & J. Underwood (Eds.), *Distributing educational resources within nations, states, school districts, and schools.* Cambridge, MA: Ballinger.

Boyd, W. L., & Kerchner, C. T. (Eds.). (1988). *The politics of excellence and choice in education.* New York: Falmer Press.

Boyd, W. L., & Walberg, H. J. (Eds.). (1990). *Choice in education: Potential and problems.* Berkeley: McCutchan.

Boyer, E. L. (1983). *High school: A report on secondary education in America.* New York: Harper and Row.

Bradford, D. F., Malt, R. A., & Oates, W. F. (1969, June). The rising cost of local public services: Some evidence and reflections. *National Tax Journal, 22* (2), 195–202.

Bradley, A. (1989a, September 13). In Connecticut, moving past pencil and paper: Teachers evaluated on class behavior. *Education Week, 9*(1), 1, 22.

Bradley, A. (1989b, September 13). 3-year effort to create a new generation of teacher assessments nears completion. *Education Week, 9*(1), 23.

Bradley, A. (1989, October 18). After two tough years in Rochester, school reformers look to the future. *Education Week, 9*(7), 1, 10–12.

Bradley, A. (1989, November 1). School-restructuring efforts forcing principals to redefine their roles. *Education Week, 9*(9), 1, 12.

Bradley, A. (1989, November 15). Coca-Cola joins growing list of education benefactors. *Education Week, 9*(11), 1, 20.

Bradley, A. (1989, December 6). N.C. schools draft reform plan to gain flexibility. *Education Week, 9*(14), 16.

Bradley, A. (1990, January 17). Despite Cuomo's support, Fernandez faces uphill battle in gaining reforms. *Education Week, 9*(17), 5.

Bradley, A. (1990, March 7). Request for developing teacher assessment prepared. *Education Week, 9*(24), 11.

Bradley, A. (1990, March 28). Job actions seen as signal of discontent over funding. *Education Week, 9*(27), 11.

Bradley, A. (1990, April 4). L. A. Board adopts guidelines on school-based management. *Education Week, 9*(28), 5.

Bradley Commission on History in the Schools. (1988). *Building on a history curriculum: Guidelines for teaching history in the schools.* Washington, DC: Educational Excellence Network.

Bredeson, P. V. (1989, March). *Redefining leadership and the roles of school* principals: Responses to changes in the professional worklife of teachers. Paper presented at the annual meeting of the American Educational Research Association, San Francisco.

Bush, G. (1989, January 18). Excerpts from speech to the White House Workshop on Choice in Education. *Education Week, 8*(17), 24.

Callahan, R. E. (1962). *Education and the cult of efficiency.* Chicago: University of Chicago Press.

Campbell, A. (n.d.). *Functions in flux.* Unpublished manuscript.

Campbell, R. F., Fleming, T., Newell, L. J., & Bennion, J. W. (1987). *A history of thought and practice in educational administration.* New York: Teachers College Press.

Career-ladder pact reached. (1990, February 14). *Education Week, 9*(21), 4.

Carlson, R. (1989). *Restructuring schools.* Internal memorandum. Washington, DC Public Schools.

Carnegie Council for Adolescent Development. (1989). *Turning points.* Washington, DC: Author.

Carnegie Forum on Education and the Economy. (1986). *A Nation prepared: Teachers for the 21st century.* Washington, DC: Author.

Carnegie Foundation for the Advancement of Teaching. (1988). *Report card on school reform: The teachers speak.* Princeton, NJ: Author.

Carnoy, M., & MacDonell, J. (1990). School district restructuring in Santa Fe, New Mexico. *Educational Policy, 4*(1), 49–64.

Casner-Lotto, J. (1988, January). Expanding the teacher's role: Hammond's school improvement process. *Phi Delta Kappan, 69*(5), 349–353.

Chapman, J., & Boyd, W. L. (1986, Fall). Decentralization, devolution, and the school principal: Australian lessons on statewide educational reform. *Educational Administration Quarterly, 22*(4), 28–58.

Chubb, J. E. (1988, Winter). Why the current wave of school reform will fail. *The Public Interest,* (90), 28–49.

Chubb, J. E., & Moe, T. M. (1990). *Politics, markets, and America's schools.* Washington, DC: Brookings Institution.

Clark, D. L., Lotto, L. S., & Astuto, T. A. (1984, Summer). Effective schools and school improvement: A comparative analysis of two lines of inquiry. *Educational Administration Quarterly, 20*(3), 41–68.

Clark, D. L., & Meloy, J. M. (1989). Renouncing bureaucracy: A democratic structure for leadership in schools. In T. J. Sergiovanni & J. A. Moore (Eds.), *Schooling for tomorrow: Directing reform to issues that count.* Boston: Allyn and Bacon.

Clinton, B. (1987, July). *Speaking of leadership.* Denver: Educational Commission of the States.

Clune, W. H., & White, P. A. (1988, September). *School-based management: Institutional variation, implementation, and issues for further research.*

New Brunswick, NJ: Center for Policy Research in Education, Eagleton Institute of Politics, Rutgers University.

Cohen, D. K. (1989, May). *Can decentralization or choice improve public education?* Paper presented at the Conference on Choice and Control in American Education. Madison: University of Wisconsin-Madison.

Cohen, D. K. (1990, March). More voices in Babel? Educational research and the politics of curriculum. *Phi Delta Kappan, 71*(7), 519–522.

Cohen, D. L. (1989, June 21). Middle grades called 'powerful' shaper of adolescents: Middle schools gain with 'focus' on child. *Education Week, 8*(39), 1, 20.

Cohen, D. L. (1989, October 11). Consensus on early-childhood needs is greeted by enthusiasm, skepticism. *Education Week, 9*(6), 15.

Cohen, D. L. (1989, October 25). State standards should complement restructuring goals, NASBE argues. *Education Week, 9*(8), 8.

Cohen, D. L. (1989, December 6). First stirrings of a new trend: Multiage classrooms gain favor. *Education Week, 9*(14), 1, 13–14.

Cohen, D. L. (1990, January 10). Project seeks to hone preschool-program accreditation. *Education Week, 9*(16), 1, 14.

Cohen, M. D., March, J. G., & Olsen, J. P. (1972, March). A garbage can model of organizational choice. *Administrative Science Quarterly, 17*(1), 1–26.

Collins, D., Ross, R. A., & Ross, T. L. (1989, December). Who wants participative management? The managerial perspective. *Group and Organizational Studies, 14*(4), 422–445.

Combs, A. W. (1988, February). New assumptions for educational reform. *Educational Leadership, 45*(5), 38–40.

Committee on Policy for Racial Justice of the Joint Center for Political Studies. (1989). *Visions of a better way: A black appraisal of public schooling.* Washington, DC: Joint Center for Political Studies.

Conley, S. C. (1988, November). Reforming paper pushers and avoiding freeagents: The teacher as a constrained decisionmaker. *Educational Administration Quarterly, 24*(4), 393–404.

Conley, S. C. (1989, March). *Who's on first? School reform, teacher participation, and the decision-making process.* Paper presented at the annual meeting of the American Educational Research Association, San Francisco.

Conway, J. A., & Jacobson, S. L. (1990). An epilogue: Where is educational leadership going? In S. L. Jacobson & J. A. Conway (Eds.), *Educational leadership in an age of reform.* New York: Longman.

Coombs, F. S. (1987, April). *The effects of increased state control on local school district governance.* Paper presented at the annual meeting of the American Educational Research Association, Washington, DC.

Coons, J. E., & Sugarman, S. D. (1978). *Education by choice.* Berkeley: University of California Press.

Cooper, B. S. (1989, November 8). Education reform in Britain. *Education Week, 9*(10), 32.

Corbett, H. D., Firestone, W. A., & Rossman, G. B. (1987, November). Resistance to planned change and the sacred in school cultures. *Educational Administration Quarterly, 23*(4), 36–59.

Corcoran, T. B. (1989). Restructuring education: A new vision at Hope Essential High School. In J. M. Rosow & R. Zager (Eds.), *Allies in educational reform.* San Francisco: Jossey-Bass Publishers.

Council of Chief State School Officers. (1989). *Success for all in a new cen-*adolescents: Middle schools gain with 'focus' on child. *Education Week, 8*(39), 1, 20.

Cohen, D. L. (1989, October 11). Consensus on early-childhood needs is greeted by enthusiasm, skepticism. *Education Week, 9*(6), 15.

Cuban, L. (1989, June). The "at-risk" label and the problem of urban school reform. *Phi Delta Kappan, 70*(10) 780–784, 799–801.

Cuban, L. (1990, January-February). Reforming again, again, and again. *Educational Researcher, 19*(1), 3–13.

Cunningham, L. L. (1989, April 11). *The Ohio State University interprofessional education program.* Presentation at Vanderbilt University, Nashville, TN.

Dade County Public Schools. (1989). *Renaissance in education.* Miami: Author.

David, J. L. (1989a). *Restructuring in progress: Lessons from pioneering districts.* Washington, DC: National Governors' Association.

David, J. L. (1989b, May). Synthesis of research on school-based management. *Educational Leadership, 46*(8), 45–53.

David, J. L., Cohen, M., Honetschlager, D., & Traiman, S. (1990). *State actions to restructure schools: First steps.* Washington, DC: National Governors' Association.

Deal, T. E. (1986). Educational change: Revival tent, tinkertoys, jungle, or carnival? In A. Lieberman (Ed.). *Rethinking school improvement: Research, craft, and concept.* New York: Teachers College Press.

Deal, T. E. (1990, May). Reframing reform. *Educational Leadership, 47*(8), 6–12.

Deal, T. E., & Kennedy, A. (1982). *Corporate cultures.* Reading, MA: Addison-Wesley.

Dokecki, P. R. (1990, May). On knowing the person as agent in caring relations. *Person-Centered Review, 5*(2), 155–169.

Downs, A. (1967). *Inside bureaucracy.* Boston: Little, Brown.

Education Commission of the States. (1983). *Action for excellence.* Denver: Author.

Elam, S. M. (1989, June). The second Gallup/Phi Delta Kappa poll of teachers' attitudes toward the public schools. *Phi Delta Kappan, 70*(10), 785–798.

Elmore, R. F. (1979–80, Winter). Backward mapping: Implementation research and policy decisions. *Political Science Quarterly, 94*(4), 601–616.

Elmore, R. F. (1987, November). Reform and the culture of authority in schools. *Educational Administration Quarterly, 23*(4), 60–78.

Elmore, R. F. (1988a). *Early experiences in restructuring schools: Voices from the field.* Washington, DC: National Governors' Association.

Elmore, R. F. (1988b). Choice in public education. In W. L. Boyd & C. T. Kerchner (Eds.). *The politics of excellence and choice in education.* New York: Falmer Press.

Elmore, R. F. (1989, March). *Models of restructured schools.* Paper presented at the annual meeting of the American Educational Research Association, San Francisco.

Ericson, D. P., & Ellett, F. S. (1989, March). *The question of the student in educational reform.* Paper presented at the annual meeting of the American Educational Research Association, San Francisco.

Evertson, C., Murphy, J., & Radnofsky, M. (1990, April). *Restructured schools: Links to the classroom.* Paper presented at the annual meeting of the American Educational Research Association, Boston.

Fernandez, J. A. (1989). *Dade County Public Schools: Blueprint for restructured schools.* Paper presented at the Conference on Choice and Control in American Education. Madison: University of Wisconsin-Madison.

Finn, C. E. (1990, April). The biggest reform of all. *Phi Delta Kappan, 71*(8), 584–592.

Finn, C. E., & Clements, S. K. (1989, July). *Reconnoitering Chicago's school reform efforts: Some early impressions.* Washington, DC: The Educational Excellence Network.

Firestone, W. A., Fuhrman, S., & Kirst, M. W. (1990). An overview of educational reform since 1983. In J. Murphy (Ed.), *The reform of American public education in the 1980s: Perspectives and cases.* Berkeley: McCutchan.

Firestone, W. A., & Wilson, B. L. (1985, July). *Management and organizational outcomes: The effects of approach and environment in schools.* Philadelphia: Research for Better Schools, Inc.

Fisher, C. W. (1990, January). The research agenda project as prologue. *Journal for Research in Mathematics Education, 21*(1), 81–89.

Flax, E. (1989, February 15). South Carolina considering "flexibility" for high-scoring schools. *Education Week, 8*(21), 1, 14.

Flax, E. (1989, November 22). S.C. board adopts regulatory relief for top-scoring schools. *Education Week, 9*(12), 1, 16.

Flax, E. (1990, May 23). Citibank pledges 20 million for school programs. *Education Week, 9*(35), 5.

Friedman, M. (1955). The role of government in education. In R. A. Salo (Ed.), *Economics and the public interest.* New Brunswick, NJ: Rutgers University Press.

Frymier, J. (1987, September). Bureaucracy and the neutering of teachers. *Phi Delta Kappan, 69*(1), 9–14.

Ginsberg, R., & Wimpelberg, R. K. (1987, Winter). Educational change by commission: Attempting "trickle down" reform. *Educational Evaluation and Policy Analysis, 9*(4), 344–360.

Giroux, H. A. (1988). *Teachers as intellectuals: Toward a critical pedagogy of learning.* Granby, MA: Bergin & Garvey.

Gomez, J. J. (1989, April). *Common problems and solutions in the implementation of school-based management.* Paper presented at the annual meeting of the American Educational Research Association, San Francisco.

Good, T. L., & Marshall, S. (1984). Do students learn more in heterogeneous or homogeneous groups? In P. L. Peterson, L. C. Wilkinson, & M. Hallinon (Eds.), *The social context of instruction: Group organization and group processes.* Orlando, FL: Academic Press.

Goodlad, J. I. (1984). *A place called school: Prospects for the future.* New York: McGraw-Hill.

Goodlad, J. I., Soder, R., & Sirotnik, K. A. (1990). *The moral dimensions of teaching.* San Francisco: Jossey-Bass.

Green, J. (1987). *The next wave: A synopsis of recent education reform reports.* Denver: Education Commission of the States.

Guthrie, J. W. (1986, December). School-based management: The next needed education reform. *Phi Delta Kappan, 68*(4), 305–309.

Guthrie, J. W., & Kirst, M. W. (1988, March). *Conditions of education in California 1988.* Berkeley: Policy Analysis for California Education. (Policy Paper No. 88–3–2).

Hallinger, P., & Richardson, D. (1988, Summer). Models of shared leadership: Evolving structures and relationships. *The Urban Review, 20*(4), 229–246.

Hampel, R. L. (1986). *The last little citadel: American high schools since 1940.* Boston: Houghton Mifflin.

Harrison, C. R., Killion, J. P., & Mitchell, J. E. (1989, May). Site-based management: The realities of implementation. *Educational Leadership, 46*(8), 55–58.

Harvey, G., & Crandall, D. P. (1988). A beginning look at the what and how of restructuring. In C. Jenks (Ed.), *The redesign of education: A collection of papers concerned with comprehensive educational reform.* San Francisco: Far West Laboratory.

Hawley, W. D. (1988, November). Missing pieces of the educational reform agenda: Or why the first and second waves may miss the boat. *Educational Administration Quarterly, 24*(4), 416–437.

Hawley, W. D. (1989). Looking backward at educational reform. *Education Week, 9*(9), 32–35.

Heifetz, R. (1988, October). Face-to-face: Leadership expert Ronald Heifetz. *INC., 10*(10), 36–48.

Holmes Group (1986, April). *Tomorrow's teachers.* East Lansing, MI: Author.

Houston, H. M. (1989, March). *Professional development for restructuring: Analyses and recommendations.* Paper presented at the annual meeting of the American Educational Research Association, San Francisco.

Jackson, K. T. (1988). *Building a history curriculum: Guidelines for teaching history in schools.* Washington, DC: Educational Excellence Network.

Jennings, L. (1989, May 10). Kean unveils proposal to experiment with three varieties of school choice. *Education Week, 8*(33), 9.

Jennings, L. (1989, June 21). Privacy rights and public-safety concerns: Debate stirs over access to youth records. *Education Week, 8,*(39), 1, 8–9.

Jennings, L. (1990, February 14). States should require schools to craft family-support plans, chiefs propose. *Education Week, 9*(21), 8.

Jordan, K. F., & McKeown, M. P. (1990). State fiscal policy and educational reform. In J. Murphy (Ed.), *The educational reform movement of the 1980s: Perspectives and Cases.* Berkeley: McCutchan.

Kearnes, D. L. (1988a, April 20). A business perspective on American schooling. *Education Week, 7*(30), 32, 24.

Kearnes, D. L. (1988b, April). An education recovery plan for America. *Phi Delta Kappan, 69* (8), 565–570.

Kerchner, C. T. (1988, November). Bureaucratic entrepreneurship: The implications of choice for school administrations. *Educational Administration Quarterly, 24*(4), 381–392.

Kerchner, C. T. (1989, April). *Trust agreements.* Paper presented at the annual meeting of the American Educational Research Association, San Francisco.

Kerchner, C. T., & Boyd, W. L. (1988). What doesn't work: An analysis of market and bureaucratic failure in schooling. In C. T. Kerchner & W. L. Boyd (Eds.), *The politics of excellence and choice in education.* New York: Falmer Press.

Kirst, M. W. (1987, October). PEER, An interview with Michael Kirst. *Phi Delta Kappan, 60*(2), 161–164.

Kirst, M. W. (Ed.). (1989). *Conditions of children in California.* Berkeley: Policy Analysis for California Education.

Kirst, M. W., McLaughlin, M., & Massell, D. (1989). *Rethinking children's policy: Implications for educational administration.* Center for Educational Research at Stanford, School of Education, Stanford University, Stanford, CA.

Le Tendre, B. (1990, April). *Implementing accelerated schools: Issues at the state level.* Paper presented at the annual meeting of the American Educational Research Association, Boston.

Levin, H. M. (1984, Summer). About time for educational reform. *Educational Evaluation and Policy Analysis, 6*(2), 151–163.

Levin, H. M. (1987, March). Accelerated schools for disadvantaged students. *Educational Leadership, 44*(6), 19–21.

Levin, H. M. (1988, Spring). Cost-effectiveness and educational policy. *Educational Evaluation and Policy Analysis, 10*(1), 51–69.

Lindelow, J. (1981). School-based management. In S. C. Smith, J. A. Mazzerella, & P. K. Piele (Eds.), *School leadership: Handbook for survival.* Eugene, OR: ERIC Clearing House on Educational Management, University of Oregon.

Lindquist, K. M., & Muriel, J. J. (1989, August). School-based management: Doomed to failure? *Education and Urban Society, 21*(4), 403–416.

Lipsitz, J. (1984). *Successful schools for young adolescents.* New Brunswick, NJ: Transaction Books.

Little, J. W. (1982, Fall). Norms of collegiality and experimentation: Work place conditions of school success. *American Educational Research Journal, 19*(3), 325–340.

Little, J. W. (1989, Summer). District policy choices and teachers' professional development opportunities. *Educational Evaluation and Policy Analysis, 11*(2), 165–179.

Lomotey, K., & Swanson, A. D. (1990). Restructuring school governance: Learning from the experiences of rural and urban schools. In S. J. Jacobson and J. A. Conway (Eds.), *Educational leadership in an age of reform.* White Plains, NY: Longman.

Lortie, D. C. (1975). *Schoolteacher.* Chicago: University of Chicago Press.

Lotto, L. S. (1983, Winter). Believing is seeing. *Organizational Theory Dialogue, 3*(1), 6–26.

Maccoby, M. (1988, November-December). A new model for leadership. *Research Technology Management, 31*(6), 53–54.

Maccoby, M. (1989, December). *Looking for leadership now.* Paper presented at the National Center for Educational Leadership conference. Harvard University, Cambridge, MA.

Malen, B., & Hart, A. W. (1987, April). *Shaping career ladder reform: The influence of teachers on the policy making process.* Paper presented at the annual meeting of the American Educational Research Association, Washington, DC.

Malen, B., & Ogawa, R. T. (1988, Winter). Professional-patron influence on site-based governance councils: A confounding case study. *Educational Evaluation and Policy Analysis, 10*(4), 251–270.

Malen, B., Ogawa, R. T., & Kranz, J. (1989, May). *What do we know about school based management? A case study of the literature—a call for research.* Paper presented at the Conference on Choice and Control in American Education. Madison: University of Wisconsin-Madison.

Maxwell, J. A., & Aronson, J. R. (1977). *Financing state and local governments* (3rd ed.). Washington, DC: The Brookings Institute.

McCarthy, M. M. (1990). Teacher testing programs. In J. Murphy (Ed.), *The educational reform movement of the 1980s: Perspectives and cases.* Berkeley: McCutchan.

McCarthey, S. J., & Peterson, P. L. (1989, March). *Teacher roles: Weaving new patterns in classroom practice and school organization.* Paper presented at the annual meeting of the American Educational Research Association, San Francisco.

McLaughlin, M. W. (1987, Summer). Learning from experience: Lessons from policy implementation. *Educational Evaluation and Policy Analysis, 9*(2), 171–178.

McNeil, L. M. (1988a, January). Contradictions of control, part 1: Administrators and teachers. *Phi Delta Kappan, 69*(5), 333–339.

McNeil, L. M. (1988b, February). Contradictions of control, part 2: Teachers, students, and curriculum. *Phi Delta Kappan, 69*(6), 432–438.

McNeil, L. M. (1988c, March). Contradictions of control, part 3: Contradictions of reform. *Phi Delta Kappan, 69*(7), 478–485.

Meyer, J. W., & Rowan, B. (1975). *Notes on the structure of educational organizations: Revised version.* Paper presented at the annual meeting of the American Sociological Association, San Francisco.

Miller, J. A. (1989, April 19). Bush floats plan to free schools from regulation. *Education Week, 8*(30), 1, 19.

Miller, J. A. (1989, May 24). Deregulation proposals move on the fast track. *Education Week, 8*(35), 11.

Miller, J. A. (1989, October 4). Educational summit's promise: "Social compact" for reforms. *Education Week, 9*(5), 1, 10.

Miller, J. A. (1989, October 11). Summit agenda likely to spark fight in congress. *Education Week, 9*(6), 1, 14.

Miller, J. A. (1989, November 22). Proposal for regulatory flexibility gains new life. *Education Week, 9*(12), 17.

Miller, S. K., & Brookover, W. B. (1986, April). *School effectiveness versus individual differences: Paradigmatic perspectives on the legitimation of economic and educational inequalities.* Paper presented at the annual meeting of the American Educational Research Association, San Francisco.

Mitchell, B. (1990). Loss, belonging and becoming: Social policy themes for children and schools. In B. Mitchell & L. L. Cunningham (Eds.), *Educational leadership and changing contexts of families, communities, and schools.* Chicago: University of Chicago Press.

Mitchell, D. E. (1989). Alternative approaches to labor-management relations for public school teachers and administrators. In J. Hannaway & R. Crowson (Eds.). *The politics of reforming school administration.* New York: Falmer Press.

Mitchell, D. E., & Encarnation, D. J. (1984, May). Alternative state policy mechanisms for influencing school performance. *Educational Researcher, 13*(5), 4–11.

Mojkowski, C., & Fleming, D. (1988, May). *School-site management: Concepts and approaches.* Andover, MA: Regional Laboratory for Educational Improvement of the Northeast and Islands.

Moore-Johnson, S. (1988, June). Pursuing professional reform in Cincinnati. *Phi Delta Kappan, 69*(10), 746–751.

Moore-Johnson, S. (1989, May). *Teachers, power, and school change.* Paper presented at the Conference on Choice and Control in American Education. Madison: University of Wisconsin-Madison.

Morgan, G. (1986). *Images of organization.* Beverly Hills, CA: Sage.

Murphy, J. (1988, Summer). Methodological measurement and conceptual problems in the study of instructional leadership. *Educational Evaluation and Policy Analysis, 10*(2), 117–139.

Murphy, J. (1989a, Fall). Educational reform in the 1980s: Explaining some surprising success. *Educational Evaluation and Policy Analysis, 11*(3), 209–221.

Murphy, J. (1989b, September 18). *Educational reform and educational equity.* Presentation made to the College of Education, Monash University, Victoria, Australia.

Murphy, J. (1989c, Fall). Educational reform and equity: A reexamination of prevailing thought. *Planning and Changing, 20*(3), 172–179.

Murphy, J. (1990a). The educational reform movement of the 1980s: A comprehensive analysis. In J. Murphy (Ed.), *The reform of American public education in the 1980s: Perspectives and cases.* Berkeley: McCutchan.

Murphy, J. (Ed.). (1990b). *The reform of American public education in the 1980s: Perspectives and cases.* Berkeley: McCutchan.

Murphy, J. (1990c). The reform of school administration: Pressures and calls for change. In J. Murphy (Ed.), *The reform of American public education in the 1980s: Perspectives and cases.* Berkeley: McCutchan.

Murphy, J. (1990d). Preparing school administrators for the 21st century: The reform agenda. In B. Mitchell & L. L. Cunningham (Eds.), *Educational leadership and changing contexts of families, communities, and schools.* Chicago: University of Chicago Press.

Murphy, J. (1990e). Principal instructional leadership. In P. W. Thurston & L. S. Lotto (Eds.), *Recent advances in educational administration* (Vol. IB). Greenwich, CT: JAI Press.

Murphy, J. (1990, September-October). Helping teachers work in restructured schools. *Journal of Teacher Education, 41*(4), 50–56.

Murphy, J. & Evertson, C. (1990). *Restructuring schools: Looking at the teaching-learning process.* Nashville, TN: George Peabody College of Education, Vanderbilt University, National Center for Educational Leadership.

Murphy, J., Evertson, C., & Radnofsky, M. (in press). Restructuring schools: Fourteen elementary and secondary teachers' proposals for reform. *Elementary School Journal.*

Murphy, J., & Hallinger, P. (1989, March-April). Equity as access to learning: Curricular and instructional treatment differences. *Journal of Curriculum Studies, 21*(2), 129–149.

Murphy, J., Hallinger, P., Lotto, L. S., & Miller, S. K. (1987, December). Barriers to implementing the instructional leadership role. *Canadian Administrator, 27*(3), 1–9.

Murphy, J., Hallinger, P., & Mesa, R. P. (1985, Summer). School effectiveness: Checking progress and assumptions and developing a role for state and federal government. *Teachers College Record, 86*(4), 615–641.

Murphy, J., Hallinger, P., & Mitman, A. (1983, Fall). Problems with research on educational leadership: Issues to be addressed. *Educational Evaluation and Policy Analysis, 5*(3), 297–305.

Murphy, J., Hull, T., & Walker, A. (1987, July-August). Academic drift and curricular debris: An analysis of high school course-taking patterns with implications for local policy makers. *Journal of Curriculum Studies, 19*(4), 341–360.

Murphy, J., Mesa, R. P., & Hallinger, P. (1984, October). A stronger state role in school reform. *Educational Leadership, 42*(2), 20–26.

Murphy, J. T. (1989, June). The paradox of decentralizing schools: Lessons from business, government, and the Catholic Church. *Phi Delta Kappan, 70*(10), 808–812.

Murphy, M. J., & Hart, A. W. (1988, October). *Preparing principals to lead in restructured schools.* Paper presented at the annual meeting of the University Council for Educational Administration, Cincinnati.

Meyer, J. W., & Rowan, B. (1975). *Notes on the structure of educational organizations. Revised version.* Paper presented at the annual meeting of the American Sociological Association, San Francisco.

National Center for Effective Schools Research and Development. (1989). *A conversation between James Comer and Ronald Edmonds: Fundamentals of effective school improvement.* Dubuque, IA: Kendall/Hunt.

National Commission for Excellence in Teacher Education. (1985). *A call for change in teacher education.* Washington, DC: American Association for Colleges for Teacher Education.

National Commission on Excellence in Education. (1983, April). *A nation at risk: The imperative of educational reform.* Washington, DC: U.S. Government Printing Office.

National Commission on Excellence in Educational Administration. (1987). *Leaders for America's schools.* Tempe, AZ: University Council for Educational Administration.

National Commission on Social Studies in the Schools. (1989). *Charting a course: Social studies for the 21st century.* Washington, DC: Author.

National Governors' Association. (1986). *Time for results.* Washington, DC: Author.

National Governors' Association. (1987). *The Governors' 1991 report on education—time for results: 1987.* Washington, DC: Author.

National Governors' Association. (1989). *Results in education 1989.* Washington, DC: Author.

National Science Board. (1983). *Educating Americans for the 21st century.* Washington, DC: National Science Board, National Science Foundation.

Newman, F. (1989). *Beyond standardized testing: Assessing authentic academic achievement in the secondary school.* Reston, VA: National Association of Secondary School Principals.

Newmann, F. M., Rutter, R. A., & Smith, M. S. (1989, October). Organizational factors that affect school sense of efficacy, community, and expectations. *Sociology of Education, 62,* 221–238.

Oakes, J. (1985). *Keeping track: How schools structure inequality.* New Haven, CT: Yale University Press.

Oakes, J., & Lipton, M. (1990, March). Examining curriculum in "best" schools. *Education Week, 9*(24), 36.

Oates, W. E. (1972). *Fiscal federalism.* New York: Harcourt Brace Jovanovich, Inc.

Odden, A. (1990). School funding changes in the 1980s. *Educational Policy, 4*(1), 33–47.

Odden, A., & Marsh, D. (1988, April). How comprehensive reform legislation can improve secondary schools. *Phi Delta Kappan, 69*(8), 593–598.

Olson, L. (1988, May 18). In Santa Fe experiment, teachers find and select their principal. *Education Week. 7*(34), 1, 20–21.

Olson, L. (1990, April 11). Unexpectedly little interest found in state offers to waive key rules. *Education Week, 9*(29), 1, 19.

O'Neil, J. (1989, November). Social studies: Charting a course for a field adrift. *ASCD Curriculum Update.*

Page, R. N. (1984, April). *Lower-track classes at a college-preparatory high school: A caricature of educational encounters.* Paper presented at the annual meeting of the American Educational Research Association, New Orleans.

Passow, A. H. (1984, April). *Reforming schools in the 1980s: A critical review of the national reports.* New York: Teachers College, Columbia University, Institute for Urban and Minority Education.

Passow, A. H. (1988, August). Whither (or Wither?) school reform? *Educational Administration Quarterly, 24*(3), 241–245.

Perry, N. J. (1988, July 4). The education crisis: What business can do. *Fortune,* 38–41.

Peters, T. J., & Waterman, R. H. (1982). *In search of excellence: Lessons from America's best run companies.* New York: Harper & Row.

Petrie, H. G. (1990). Reflections on the second wave of reform: Restructuring the teaching profession. In S. L. Jacobson & J. A. Conway (Eds.), *Educational leadership in an age of reform.* New York: Longman.

Pipho, C. (1989, February 1). Switching labels: From vouchers to choice. *Education Week, 8*(19), 27.

Plank, D. N. (1987, June). *Why school reform doesn't change schools: Political and organizational perspectives.* Paper presented at the annual meeting of the American Educational Research Association, Washington, DC.

Plank, D. N., & Ginsberg, R. (1990). Catch the wave: Reform commissions and school reform. In J. Murphy (Ed.), *The reform of American public education in the 1980s: Perspectives and cases.* Berkeley: McCutchan.

Porter, A. C. (1988, April). *External standards and good teaching: The pros and cons of telling teachers what to do.* Paper presented at the annual meeting of the American Educational Research Association, New Orleans.

Powell, A. G., Farrar, E., & Cohen, D. K. (1985). *The shopping mall high school: Winners and losers in the educational marketplace.* Boston: Houghton-Mifflin.

Purpel, D. E. (1989). *The moral and spiritual crises in education: A curriculum for justice and compassion in education.* Granby, MA: Bergin & Garvey.

Quality Education for Minorities Project. (1990). *Education that works: An action plan for the education of minorities.* Cambridge, MA: Massachusetts Institute of Technology.

Radnofsky, M. L., Evertson, C. M., & Murphy, J. (1990, April). *Restructured schools, tracking classroom effects: Teachers' perceptions.* Paper presented at the annual meeting of the American Educational Research Association, Boston.

Rallis, S. F. (1990). Professional teachers and restructured schools: Leadership challenges. In B. Mitchell & L. L. Cunningham (Eds.), *Educational leadership and changing contexts of families, communities, and schools.* Chicago: University of Chicago Press.

Resnick, D. P., & Resnick, L. B. (1985, April). Standards, curriculum, and performance: A historical and comparative perspective. *Educational Researcher, 14*(4), 5–20.

Rosenholtz, S. J. (1985, May). Effective schools: Interpreting the evidence. *American Journal of Education, 93*(2), 352–389.

Rothman, R. (1989, May 17). What to teach: Reform turns finally to the essential question. *Education Week, 8*(34), 1, 8, 10.

Rothman, R. (1989, June 21). San Diego adds Socratic seminars to teacher repertoires. *Education Week, 8*(39), 5.

Rothman, R. (1989, September 13). In Connecticut, moving past pencil and paper: Student assessment rates performance. *Education Week, 9*(1), 1, 21.

Rothman, R. (1989a, October 11). In an effort to boost achievement, Denver abolishes remedial classes. *Education Week, 9*(6), 1, 27.

Rothman, R. (1989b, October 11). California panel backs science curriculum that includes evolution as a major theme. *Education Week, 9*(6), 17.

Rothman, R. (1989, October 25). Ford creates $10-million program for middle-school math. *Education Week, 9*(8), 5.

Rothman, R. (1990, January 24). NAEP will make its most extensive use of performance items. *Education Week, 9*(18), 1, 21.

Rothman, R. (1990, February 14). Aiming for "definition of literacy," NAEP considers 1992 reading test. *Education Week, 9*(21), 1, 22.

Schlechty, P. C. (1990). *Schools for the twenty-first century: Leadership imperatives for educational reform.* San Francisco: Jossey-Bass.

Schmidt, P. (1989, November 22). Foundation formed to spur partnerships to create business-school "academies." *Education Week, 9*(12), 14.

Schmidt, P. (1990, February 14). Sobol seeks plan that focuses more on other cultures. *Education Week, 9*(21), 9.

Sedlak, M. W., Wheeler, C. W., Pullin, D. C., & Cusick, P. A. (1986). *Selling students short: Classroom bargains and academic reform in the American high school.* New York: Teachers College Press.

Seeley, D. S. (1980, February). *The bankruptcy of service delivery.* Paper presented at the Foundation Lunch Group: Panel on Children, at the Edwin Gould Foundation for Children, New York City.

Seeley, D. S. (1988, February). A new vision for public education. *Youth Policy, 10*(2), 34–36.

Sergiovanni, T. J. (1989). The leadership needs for quality schooling. In T. J. Sergiovanni & J. H. Moore (Eds.), *Schooling for tomorrow: Directing reforms to issues that count.* Boston: Allyn & Bacon.

Sergiovanni, T. J., Burlingame, M., Coombs, F. S., & Thurston, P. W. (1987). *Educational governance and administration* (2nd ed.). Englewood Cliffs, NJ: Prentice-Hall.

17,000 file for school-council seats in Chicago. (1989, October 11). *Education Week, 9*(6), 5.

Shepard, L. A., & Kreitzer, A. E. (1987, August-September). The Texas teacher test. *Educational Researcher, 16*(6), 22–31.

Short, P. M., & Greer, J. T. (1989, March). *Increasing teacher autonomy through shared governance: Effects on policy making and student outcomes.* Paper presented at the American Educational Research Association, San Francisco.

Sickler, J. L. (1988, January). Teachers in charge: Empowering the professionals. *Phi Delta Kappan, 69*(5), 354–356, 375–376.

Sirotnik, K. A. (1989). The school as the center of change. In T. J. Sergiovanni & J. H. Moore (Eds.). *Schooling for tomorrow: Directing reforms to issues that count.* Boston: Allyn & Bacon.

Sizer, T. R. (1984). *Horace's compromise: The dilemma of the American high school.* Boston: Houghton Mifflin.

Slavin, R. E. (1988, October). On research and school organization: A conversation with Bob Slavin. *Educational Leadership, 46*(2), 22–29.

Slavin, R. E. (1990, January 18). *Successful programs for at risk students.* Paper presented at the Vanderbilt Institute for Policy Studies, Vanderbilt University, Nashville, TN.

Smylie, M. A., & Denny, J. W. (1989, March). *Teacher leadership: Tensions and ambiguities in organizational perspective.* Paper presented at the annual meeting of the American Educational Research Association, San Francisco.

Snider, W. (1989, February 8). Milwaukee to decentralize management of schools. *Education Week, 8*(20), 7.

Snider, W. (1989, March 1). "Personalizing" high schools. *Education Week, 8*(23), 1, 6–7.

Snider, W. (1989, November 1). Known for choice, New York's District 4 offers a complex tale for urban reformers. *Education Week, 9*(9), 1, 13.

Snider, W. (1989, December 13). California district makes choice initiative centerpiece of plan to reinvigorate schools. *Education Week, 9*(15), 1, 22.

Snider, W. (1990, January 31). Rockefeller project targets needs of at-risk students. *Education Week, 9*(19), 6.

Snider, W. (1990, March 14). Chicago councils begin to decide fate of principals. *Education Week, 9*(25), 1, 13.

Snider, W. (1990, April 11). Washington lawmakers adopt school-choice package. *Education Week, 9*(29), 14.

Soltis, J. F. (1988, August). Reform or reformation? *Educational Administration Quarterly, 24*(3), 241–245.

Southern Regional Education Board. (1990). *Educational benchmarks 1990.* Atlanta: Author.

Spady, W. G. (1988, October). Organizing for results: The basis of authentic restructuring and reform. *Educational Leadership, 46*(2), 4–8.

State Capitals (1989, October 11). *Education Week, 9*(6), 19.

Sykes, G., & Elmore, R. F. (1989). Making schools more manageable. In J. Hannaway & R. L. Crowson (Eds.), *The politics of reforming school administrations.* New York: Falmer Press.

Text of final summit statement issued by President, Governors (1989, October 4). *Education Week, 9*(5), 12.

Thompson, J. A. (1988). The second wave of educational reform: Implications for school leadership, administration, and organization. In F. C. Wendel & M. T. Bryant (Eds.), *New directions for administration preparation.* Tempe, AZ: The University Council for Educational Administration.

Timar, T. B., & Kirp, D. L. (1988, Summer). State efforts to reform schools: Treading between a regulatory swamp and an English garden. *Educational Evaluation and Policy Analysis, 10*(2), 75–88.

Tyack, D. B. (1974). *One best system.* Cambridge, MA: Harvard University Press.

Tyack, D. B., & Hansot, E. (1982). *Managers of virtue: Public school leadership in America, 1920–1989.* New York: Basic Books.

Underwood, J. (1990). State legislative responses to educational reform literature. In P. W. Thurston & L. S. Lotto (Eds.), *Recent advances in educational administration* (Vol. IA). Greenwich, CT: JAI Press.

United States Department of Education (1989). *Educating our children: Parents and schools together.* Washington, DC: Author.

Viadero, D. (1989, September 13). Citing "flexibility," schools float plan to hire teachers from private firms. *Education Week, 9*(1), 7.

Viadero, D. (1989, November 1). L. A. school embraces a West German import. *Education Week, 9*(9), 1, 10.

Viadero, D. (1989, November 15). Chiefs propose guidelines to assist in restructuring. *Education Week, 9*(11), 6.

Wagstaff, L. H., & Gallagher, K. S. (1990). Schools, families, and communities: Idealized images and new realities. In B. Mitchell & L. L. Cunningham (Eds.), *Educational leadership and changing contexts of families, communities, and schools.* Chicago: University of Chicago Press.

Walker, R. (1989, November 8). Business leaders challenge Bush's school priorities. *Education Week, 9*(10), 1, 23.

Walker, R. (1989, December 6). Decisive legislative battle on choice looms in California. *Education Week, 9*(14), 15.

Walsh, M. (1990, May 23). Colorado lawmakers mandate open enrollment within districts. *Education Week, 9*(35), 11.

Warren, D. (1990). Passage of rites: On the history of educational return in the United States. In J. Murphy (Ed.), *The educational return movement of the 1980s: Perspectives and cases.* Berkeley: McCutchan.

Watkins, J. M., & Lusi, S. F. (1989). *Facing the essential tensions: Restructuring from where you are.* Paper presented at the annual meeting of the American Educational Research Association, San Francisco.

Watt, J. (1989). The devolution of power: The ideological meaning. *Journal of Educational Administration, 27*(1), 19–28.

Wehlage, G. G., Rutter, R. A., & Turnbaugh, A. (1987, March). A program model for at-risk high school students. *Educational Leadership, 44*(6), 70–73.

Weick, K. E. (1976, March). Educational organizations as loosely coupled systems. *Administrative Science Quarterly, 21*(1), 1–19.

Weick, K. E., & McDaniel, R. R. (1989). How professional organizations work: Implications for school organization and management. In T. J. Sergiovanni & J. H. Moore (Eds.), *Schooling for tomorrow: Directing reforms to issues that count.* Boston: Allyn & Bacon.

Weis, J. G., & Hawkins, J. D. (1979, December). *Background paper for delinquency prevention research and development program.* Seattle: University of Washington, National Center for the Assessment of Delinquent Behavior and Its Prevention.

Wise, A. E. (1978, February). The hyper-rationalization of American education. *Educational Leadership, 35*(5), 354–361.

Wise, A. E. (1989). Professional teaching: A new paradigm for the management of education. In T. J. Sergiovanni & J. H. Moore (Eds.). *Schooling for tomorrow: Directing reforms to issues that count.* Boston: Allyn & Bacon.

Wise, A. E. (1989, October 18). Calling for "National Institutes of Education." *Education Week, 9*(7), 36.

Zeichner, K. M. (1989, Spring). Preparing teachers for democratic schools. *Action in Teacher Education, 11*(1), 5–10.

Index

About the Author

Joseph Murphy is Professor and Chair, the Department of Educational Leadership, Peabody College of Vanderbilt University. He is also a Senior Research Fellow with the National Center for Educational Leadership. His work focuses on the issue of school improvement, with particular interest in the role that school administrators can play in that process.